IRONDAD LIFE

A Year of Bad Decisions and Questionable Motives—
What I Learned on the Quest to Conquer Ironman Lake Placid

RUSSELL NEWELL

Post Hill
PRESS

A POST HILL PRESS BOOK
ISBN: 978-1-64293-766-4
ISBN (eBook): 978-1-64293-767-1

Irondad Life:
A Year of Bad Decisions and Questionable Motives—
What I Learned on the Quest to Conquer Ironman Lake Placid
© 2021 by Russell Newell
All Rights Reserved

Cover art by Cody Corcoran

Post Hill Press
New York • Nashville
posthillpress.com

Published in the United States of America
Printed in Canada

To Karoline—
thanks for putting up with me
and loving me, despite my shenanigans.

To Jim—
for getting me into most of these shenanigans
and allowing me to write about you.

TABLE OF CONTENTS

IRONMAN GLOSSARY

Aero: A position on the bike where you lean low over the handlebars to make yourself more aerodynamic and faster. Also, the best way to ensure you will have to see a chiropractor for the following six months.

Arms Race: A buildup of weapons to rival the Soviet Union and U.S. during the Reagan administration. A one-upmanship orgy that would make the Egyptian pharaohs pack up their ball and go home. I see your run coach, Zipp wheels, and Velocity Ultra wetsuit and raise you a swim coach, a Giro Vanquish MIPS Helmet, and a Cervelo P5. The reason you have to get a second job working at Foot Locker on the weekends.

Beehive: When you swim and are surrounded by other swimmers in front, back, left, and right with no place to go.

Bonking: Bonking, or "hitting the wall," is a term most athletes recognize. While it isn't something all will experience, when you bonk, you'll know it. It's unmistakable—the feeling of severe weakness, fatigue, confusion, and disorientation. You will bonk if you don't fuel your body properly. Lance Armstrong bonked during the climb up the Col de Joux Plane in the French Alps during the 2000 Tour de France and called it the worst day on the bike he'd ever had.

Brick: Method of training in which you try to simulate the race by doing two or more of the legs back-to-back. For example, you might do a fifty-mile bike ride followed by a twelve-mile run, or a mile swim followed by a bike ride or a run. These are designed to get the body used to doing two disciplines, one after another. Also, what I'll shit out of my ass at 5:30 a.m. in the porta potty before a race to clear the decks, lighten the load, drop excess cargo.

Butt Paste: Your best friend in an Ironman. See Chafing.

Catchers: People who volunteer to catch you when you cross the finish line and can no longer walk. By the time you reach the finish line, you're staggering like Rocky after the beating Mr. T puts on him. You're punch drunk, delirious, stiffer than a two-by-four board, and moving like the zombies in *The Walking Dead*. Catchers are there to hold you up and carry you out of the way of other staggering corpses. They throw a foil blanket on you to keep you warm while your body temperature plummets, throw a medal over your neck and prop you up for a finisher's photo, and then point you to the pizza or the medical tent, depending on whether you need something to eat or an IV.

Century: How old you will feel after an Ironman. Also refers to a one hundred-mile bike ride. Many people do century rides as part of their training for an Ironman.

Chafing: Chafing can happen during all three disciplines during an Ironman if you don't properly lubricate certain areas. During the swim, the wetsuit collar can rub against and irritate the neck; during the bike ride, your groin area and inner thighs rub against the seat and chafe; during the run, your nipples will get irritated by your shirt rubbing against them.

Clinchers: Can refer to the muscles you use when you're trying to hold in a shit explosion during the run, or the type of rim on the wheel of your bike. Clincher wheels, versus tubular, are the most common type and are used with a tire and an inner tube. If you get a flat tire with a clincher, you can change out the inner tube and get back on your bike quickly.

Commando: My friend Jim Kane's preferred swimming approach. In this case, it does not mean naked, thank Christ. Swimming commando means not wearing a wetsuit. You're crazy if you forgo a wetsuit for any reason. Wetsuits, made of neoprene, do three things: keep you warm(er); keep you more buoyant, meaning you don't have to work as hard to stay afloat; and help you swim faster.

Compression: Can mean either squeezing your ass cheeks as hard as you can to contain the deluge until the next porta potty, or socks, underwear, or arm sleeves that compress your muscles during an Ironman event, aiding recovery. I swear by compression socks and pants. I will never race without them.

DNF, DNS, DFL: Did Not Finish. Did Not Start. Dead Fucking Last.

Jet Stream: The warm flow you feel if you're swimming behind Jim Kane when he pees. I cannot pee and swim at the same time, so I will never be accused of jet-streaming anyone.

Mass Start: Another term for chaos. This refers to the quaint time in Ironman when they used to let nearly 3000 people all jump into a lake at the same time and start racing against each other. Picture the start of the Boston or New York City marathons: thousands of people jockeying for position, knocking into each other, pushing, shoving, all being funneled through a narrow street that is built to only fit ten at a time. The mass swim start in an Ironman is akin to a herd of water buffalo in Africa all rushing to the same body of water in panic, helter-skelter, crashing into each other, climbing over one another, eyes filled with panic, limbs flailing in fear, trying to escape the lions chasing them.

Nutrition: Your car can't run on maple syrup and Cocoa Puffs, and neither can you. Nutrition is the fuel you need to complete an Ironman. It replaces cupcakes, pizza, and beer with green stuff called vegetables, lean proteins, clean carbs, and good fats. Learn to love avocado.

PR: Personal Record. What keeps you coming back for more each year or every couple of years: that desire to break your fastest time. The justification for signing up for another race even though you're older and more brittle. If I just fix my swim stroke, I'll finish in under twelve hours this time. Definitely.

Retired: Means your next race is more than three months away. You never retire, despite proclaiming it to all your loved ones and your long-suffering spouse immediately after every race. The following morning, you and all your buddies who similarly proclaimed retirement are plotting out next year's races. A similar phenomenon to how women forget the agony of childbirth and continue having kids.

Disclaimer: Around my wife, I will deny comparing competing in an Ironman to having a baby more vehemently than Peter denied Christ.

Sherpas: Term is stolen from climbers of Mount Everest, who employ local climbers to guide them to the summit. For climbers attempting to summit Everest, Sherpas do everything from cook meals to carry oxygen to climb ahead and set the ropes. In Ironman, Sherpas are vital to summiting the Ironman course. Sherpa duties are usually carried out by a family member or friend. Sherpas retrieve your bike when you're done. They carry all your gear around for you. They get you a beer when you can't get up from the couch because your legs hurt too much.

Special Needs Bag: Really, the "just in case" bag. There is a special needs drop area for the bike and the run. You might put in a sweatshirt or a windbreaker. Maybe a pair of socks or aspirin or food. Or spare tubes, extra gels, or salt tabs. I have no idea because I've never packed a special needs bag in my ten years of doing Ironman.

Strippers: No, not Chippendales or Candy from the Cheetah Lounge. Refers to the wetsuit stripper after the swim who throws you on your back, lifts your legs up and pulls your wetsuit off—pulls so hard, you slide across the tarmac. Only thing missing is stirrups and a baby.

Tapering: The act of winding down a long training season after building up distance, endurance, and miles, lessening your workload so you have something left in the tank for the Ironman. Kind of like a bye week in football. Tapering lets the body heal and the muscles repair—at least, so I've heard. I've never done it due to time constraints that go along with having three kids under the age of five. I ramp up when others are tapering. I'm an idiot, however.

"It is not the critic who counts; not the man who points out how the strong man stumbles, or where the doer of deeds could have done them better. The credit belongs to the man who is actually in the arena, whose face is marred by dust and sweat and blood; who strives valiantly; who errs, who comes short again and again, because there is no effort without error and shortcoming; but who does actually strive to do the deeds; who knows great enthusiasms, the great devotions; who spends himself in a worthy cause; who at the best knows in the end the triumph of high achievement, and who at the worst, if he fails, at least fails while daring greatly, so that his place shall never be with those cold and timid souls who neither know victory nor defeat."

— Teddy Roosevelt

CHAPTER 1
COMBAT SWIMMING

Just keep swimming.
— Dory from *Finding Nemo*

Mile 1.6

As I bobbed in the lake, gasping for breath, swimmers crashing into me, my insides feeling like a raccoon was caught there and trying to claw his way out, I looked desperately for the nearest rescue boat.

Goddamn cayenne pepper shot.

One of the basic rules of doing an Ironman race is never, ever introduce something new to your system on race day. Ever.

I had spent $900 on a nutritionist instead of fixing my 2007 Passat, whose engine light had been on so long it now blinked, "Please drive me off a cliff and just end this already." I did this to make absolutely sure that I had a winning nutrition plan for Ironman Lake Placid. Sarah of SoMoved Nutrition had reminded me a half dozen times not to try anything new the morning of the race.

I wasn't going to make the same mistake my friend and Ironman enabler, Jim Kane, made at Mooseman Half Ironman in New Hampshire. He had what for him was a horrible swim.

"What happened?" I had asked after the race. "Your swim sucked."

"I puked. It was all over me, so I dove two feet underwater to rinse the vomit off. I had to rest there a bit to recover."

"I'm sure the people around you loved swimming in your vomit. What'd you eat this morning?"

"Three bowls of cereal with whole milk, a blueberry muffin, and orange juice. But I think the large Italian sub with everything on it, including extra hots, and the three beers I had last night was more of the issue."

"You think? Dumbass."

Fast forward to Ironman Lake Placid, 2018. Thirty minutes before I was going to rush into a freezing cold lake with 2,500 other people to swim two and a half miles, my uncle, Bob Falconi, veteran of roughly fifty Ironman races, handed me a tube.

"What's this?" I asked.

"It's cayenne pepper juice," he said. "Want some? It'll help with cramps."

Gee, I've never had this in my life. I hate spicy foods. I have no idea how my body is going to respond. And I'm about to do an Ironman. Why not? What could possibly go wrong?

But this was Uncle Bob, guru of ultra-races and Ironmans. So when he handed me the tube filled with liquid capsaicin pepper extract, I chugged it like a college freshman at a frat party handed a shot of fireball by a beautiful sorority senior.

To be fair, I had suffered cramps in every Ironman swim I'd done. If you don't know what that's like, try swimming two miles with only one leg because the other one is locked up in an agonizing spasm. Not ideal. And I don't want to hear about all the physically challenged athletes who swim with one leg or one arm or blind *every* time. I'm not mentally tough like them. As Jim has told me, "You're as soft as an overripe peach."

So be it. I prefer to have both legs working during a race, and I wanted to see what I might do if I didn't cramp up during the swim.

I had come so far in my aquatic aptitude since I started training for my first Ironman—Lake Placid 2012. Because Lake Placid Ironman sold out every year within minutes of when registration opened, Jim and I had signed up to volunteer in 2011 so that we would get priority registration and have a better chance of getting a spot in the 2012 race.

We decided we would familiarize ourselves with the course, starting with the two-loop swim in Mirror Lake. "I'm swimming a loop on Thursday at 7 a.m. if you want to join me," Uncle Bob notified us. He was racing that Sunday and had a strict routine in place the days before the race.

Jim and I were feeling quite full of ourselves. "Look at us—a full year before the race, and we're already training and familiarizing ourselves with the course. Those schmucks who won't start training for another week won't have a chance!"

On Thursday morning, we showed up in cargo shorts with deep side pockets, in which we each carried two cans of beer. We did this to ensure that they would still be cold when we finished the swim. Uncle Bob shook his head. "You two are something. You really are."

In addition to having wildly ineffective swim gear, my form in those days was—in a word—lacking. Have you ever seen a dog or a young child just learning to swim, head and neck jutting out like a scared giraffe, looking for the nearest wall or escape from the water, arms thrashing and legs churning a mile a minute while the body inches forward? That was me.

Swimming is all about form—being streamlined and efficient. It should look effortless and graceful as you glide through the water, cutting through like a Ginsu knife through one of our beer cans.

TIP: You can't win an Ironman race during the swim, but you can lose one. Slow and steady will get the job done, and you'll live to see the bike. Stay calm and swim on.

I had moved to California to work for Disney at the beginning of 2012, so I joined the Disney Tri Team to meet some people and gain some training tips. One weekend, the team sponsored a swimming class with Masters swim coach Stuart McDougal and his daughter Mandy, founders of Mind, Body, and SWIM. It was…revealing.

The first thing Stuart and Mandy did was test my stroke by filming me swimming laps at race pace. I thought I was going to have a stroke by the time I finished. I was gasping for air so hard that one would have thought I had smoked a pack of cigarettes during the swim.

I learned that I was using roughly 10,000 strokes on each lap—a few more than the fourteen I should have been taking. This, they explained, meant that I was shortening my stroke— that is, my arms were churning in short, quick bursts, reducing the length of the "pull" through the water and diminishing the distance traveled per stroke. The result was that it took me many more strokes to swim the same distance, expending way too much energy.

Stuart and Mandy taught me how the arms should fully extend in long strokes, lengthening the distance per stroke. They taught me how my hips and shoulders should rotate. They taught me to kick from the hips in compact, efficient kicks to generate power and speed.

My other big problem was that I stuck my head out of the water every second, angling my body in the most water-resistant position possible. I couldn't have created more drag had I tied a parachute to my leg. I looked nothing like a missile speeding efficiently through the water, unless missiles now moved like Nemo, the one-finned clownfish.

I took my newfound knowledge and revamped my swim stroke. I bought hand paddles to improve my form and strengthen my arms and shoulders. I no longer exhausted myself swimming two laps.

Through the years, I made other slight improvements in my swim preparation, mainly concerning learning the value of a proper wetsuit. Ironman racing is an expensive proposition, so to save money, Jim and I bought our wetsuits at Ocean State Job Lot, saving roughly $800.

I saved even more by buying a child size large for $19 instead of an adult small. We gave each other knowing glances at the lake and hoisted our beers at the bar, acknowledging how much cleverer we were than all the morons paying full price for their fancy wetsuits.

Then we noticed all those morons passing us as we took on more water than the Titanic. Their wetsuits were much more buoyant, raising the hips and legs to facilitate a more effective swimming position. They were more flexible and didn't impede arm or leg motion, encouraging better technique and more power. They were aerodynamic. They were made with a slick neoprene, low-absorption rubber rightly advertised as "lightning fast."

Those expensive wetsuits with names like Maverick X, Velocity Ultra, Aquaman, Vanquish, and Rip Curl E-bomb were designed to be buoyant, flexible, and fast. Mine was as buoyant as a brick. Mine absorbed water like a bath sponge and was two degrees more flexible than a straitjacket. Mine was designed for a twelve-year-old boy to dig clams in two-feet-deep water.

I broke down and bought an Xterra Vortex 4 for $400. This was a big improvement, though I still had issues to overcome. At Ironman Boulder in 2014, I put the wetsuit on right before the swim. It didn't feel right. It wasn't fitting properly.

"Hey, jackass," Jim said. "You might want to dial back your expectations for this swim."

"What are you talking about? I'm dialed in. You're going to drown in my wake!"

"Okay, big boy. But you might have a better chance if you figure out that your legs don't go in the arm sleeves."

I had somehow put my legs in the arm sleeves and arms in the leg sleeves. I had to scramble before the starting gun to put it on correctly.

TIP: Pay for a good wetsuit. And wear it. And learn how to put it on. Some athletes choose to swim in only a Speedo, thinking they need to pass some sort of swim-purity test. Don't be so stupid. Wetsuits, made with about a quarter inch of neoprene, do three things: keep you warm(er); keep you more buoyant, meaning you don't have to work as hard to stay afloat; and help you swim faster. I've raced with a wetsuit and with a swimsuit marketed as a speed-

suit. I swam much slower in the speedsuit and had to work much harder to achieve that slow pace. I recommend training in a bathing suit, then racing with a wetsuit. It will feel like moving from a 1940s hickory-stick golf club hitting a baseball to a Callaway Warbird slicing through a perfectly wound long-distance golf ball. Ping.

By Lake Placid 2018, I had figured a lot out in the swim. In past swims, I primarily used only my arms, theorizing that I could save my legs for the bike and the run. While this might give my legs a little more gas later, the result was a slower swim. But this year, I was feeling strong. My form was good! I was going to employ my flutter kick for the first time! I had hired a nutritionist, goddammit!!

My engine for past races had been fueled by Cocoa Puffs, pizza, and beer. Sarah had shown me the light. I had not eaten any refined sugar or processed food in weeks. I had cut my two-glasses-of-wine-with-dinner-a-night wine habit and didn't drink for six months. I wolfed down brussels sprouts and broccoli with the same zeal I had once dedicated to Talenti banana chocolate swirl gelato. I ate *clean*.

I had never finished an Ironman in under thirteen hours, but this time was going to be different. In my imagination, I'd cross the finish line in first place in my age group—somewhere in the nine- to ten-hour range—an Ironman god like Lionel Sanders, Jan Frodeno, or Daniela Ryf. Okay, maybe I'd settle for demigod. But I was going to slay!

I decided that this race, I'd flutter kick my little legs for the entire swim like super-speedy Dash in that scene from *The Incredibles*. To use a golf analogy, I was going to grip it and rip it and see what happened.

What happened was instead of going 300 yards down the middle of the fairway, my golf ball hit the nearest tree, ricocheted back, and slammed into my gut.

Here I was, a mile into the swim, trying to find the nearest rescue boat, bobbing like the Lego Stormtrooper my three-year-old had thrown into the toilet bowl before I unwittingly flushed him down. The left side of my stomach felt like someone had put my torso in a vice and begun squeezing.

I assumed it was a stomach issue brought on by the pepper shot. But what if it was something serious? For years, I had heard the family story of seven-year-old Austin Daly, my distant Irish relation who complained to his teacher of stomach pain and asked to be excused from school. She thought he was being lazy and refused.

By the time Austin got home, his appendix had burst, and it was too late. He died that afternoon before they got him to the hospital. What if my appendix was bursting? What if I was putting myself in jeopardy? Did I need to get to the hospital? What if I passed out from the pain and drowned?

Dying during the swim was not unheard of. A British woman had gone into cardiac arrest just a few months prior during the swim portion of a Half Ironman in Spain. She was rushed to the hospital where she remained brain-dead until she died the next day.

The year before, a fifty-four-year-old man became distressed two hours into the swim at Ironman Texas. He was pulled from the water, and CPR was performed on him for about twenty minutes. He was taken to a nearby hospital, where he also died.

So dying is a distinct possibility for those racing in an Ironman. And despite it being the first leg of the race and covering the shortest distance, swimming has proved to be the most likely place to perish.

One study analyzed the results of 2,971 USA Triathlon-sanctioned events held from 2006 to 2008, during which fourteen participants died—thirteen of them while swimming and one while biking. Eleven were men.[1]

Researchers conducting a study of triathlon deaths between 1985 and 2015 identified 109 cases of race-related sudden death, 12 instances of resuscitated cardiac arrests, and 15 trauma deaths.[2]

An example of a trauma death would be when a man on the bike leg of Ironman France in Nice took a steep descent at a brisker-than-recommended pace and couldn't make a turn.

---

1   Kevin M. Harris, et al, "Sudden Death During the Triathlon," *JAMA: The Journal of American Medical Association*, April 7, 2010, https://jamanetwork.com/journals/jama/fullarticle/185622.
2   Bonnie D. Ford, "Study of triathlon deaths concludes more screening needed," April 5, 2016, ESPN, https://www.espn.com/sports/endurance/story/_/id/15139696/middle-aged-male-participants-need-health-screening.

He went off the road and crashed into a wall. In the words of a local emergency services aide, "he suffered a major head injury and had a cardiac arrest...we were unable to revive him at the scene and following an emergency airlift by helicopter he died en route to the hospital."[3]

The study also found that most of the deaths and near deaths were middle-aged males. So...me. Was it my time to be flushed (wittingly) down the toilet of life?

I don't think it should really surprise anyone that if you're going to die doing an Ironman, the swim is where it will happen. Let me describe the typical Ironman jaunt in the water.

First, you're not swimming laps in a nice wide lane in a heated pool at the YMCA where you can stand or grab the side and rest every few laps. No sir. You swim in an ice-cold lake or a freezing ocean with waves and currents and jellyfish stinging you. Or, if you participated in the Ironman U.S. Championship in 2012, you swam in raw sewage after a broken sewer line dumped millions of gallons into the Hudson River.

I once swam in the Nautica Triathlon in Malibu, California, in six-foot waves. As I headed toward shore, a giant wave crashed on me and knocked me ass over teakettle. I thought I was going to drown as I washed around the bottom of the Pacific Ocean like I was in my washing machine's spin cycle.

---

3   Peter Allen, "British triathlete, 30, dies after crashing his bike into a wall during 'Ironman' in southern France," MailOnline, June 24, 2013, https://www.dailymail.co.uk/news/article-2347185/British-triathlete-30-dies-crashing-bike-wall-Ironman-southern-France.html.

You also have to contend with three thousand other people all swimming at the same time, swimming over each other, kicking each other, pulling each other, punching, and clawing. And you're not swimming a 100-meter dash. You swim 2.4 miles—far enough that your legs are so tired you can barely walk on them when you get out of the water.

By the end of the first mile, you've been kicked in the head eighteen times. You also probably lost your goggles in the first fifteen minutes, weren't able to see the markers through the fog, and swam the wrong direction for an additional mile before realizing you were swimming out to sea and needed to turn around.

TIP: Lake Placid is one of the few Ironman swims in the world that has an underwater cable on the buoy line. If you're comfortable getting knocked around, fight for the cable, and use it to help you sight where you're going and stay on course. You'll also take advantage of the pull of the current generated by all the swimmers. But be prepared for a bumpy ride. It's not for the faint of heart.

Ironman now has athletes swim in waves so that everyone isn't starting at the same time. But back in 2012, they were still using the quaint method of a mass start. Mass start is another term for chaos.

The mass start begins with athletes waiting in line to enter the water…a slow slog of people pressing up against each other like a crowd of overzealous bargain hunters pushing through the Walmart entrance on Black Friday.

Then, when the starting gun goes off, the scene resembles a herd of water buffalo in Africa all rushing to the same river in a panic, crashing into each other, climbing over one another, pushing the others down, eyes filled with fear, trying to escape the lions chasing them. And that's just entering the water.

They say the average Ironman swim takes four times more energy to complete than running the same distance. To me, the swim is the least physically taxing leg of the Ironman. But it is by far the scariest and most mentally grueling. There is good reason to be afraid.

Once you get in the water, you spend much of your time fending off the barbarian horde coming after you.

People have no qualms about grabbing your leg and pulling you back if you're in their way. I've had people swim right on top of me, pushing me down into the murky, churning breach. You will get kicked in the head, guaranteed. Your goggles may fog up, and then you might as well swim blindfolded.

TIP: To prevent your goggles from fogging, rinse them with tearless baby shampoo right before you enter the water. You may still cry like a baby, but it won't be because of the shampoo, and at least you'll be able to see.

It's hard to stay calm in the swim. And when the adrenaline is pumping and your heart is pounding out of your chest, bad things can happen.

I tried to stay calm, but I was suffering. I had a wife and three young kids. And my wife worried excessively about my well-being during races. I should also mention that she hates that I do Ironmans. She actually forbade me to do them until all our kids were out of diapers. I finally broke her, and she relented for this one last hurrah in Lake Placid. "Jim, I'm a go for LP! I got the Rocky speech from Karoline…except instead of 'just win' she said, 'don't die.'" Real inspirational stuff.

Yes, my wife Karoline's only request was that I not die. I agreed to this. No race is worth dying over. I had to think of my young family. I looked around for boats or officials in kayaks to pull me out and end the misery—and keep me from drowning.

But I knew that the minute I touched a boat or received help, I would be done for the day. I would not hear Mike Reilly announce twelve hours or so later that Russell Newell was an Ironman. And that was seemingly more important at that moment than seeing my kids grow into adulthood.

I bobbed for a few moments more and decided it was simply stomach issues caused by my stupid cayenne pepper adventure and that I had to try to make it to shore where I could rest and reassess.

Maybe if I just took a shit in my wetsuit right there in the lake, the agony would abate, and I'd be able to make it. At Ironman Boulder, I had peed while we waited in line to enter the water before the swim. I thought it would be inconspicuous enough until a yellow stream began rolling down the gravel hill toward the lake.

As the stream made its way through the feet of the people in front of me, they began looking down to see why their feet were getting wet. When they realized what it was, they turned around in disgust to confront the guilty party. So naturally, I looked down then turned around too, giving the people behind me a nasty look. *You disgust me.*

I decided peeing was one thing, but unleashing full-fledged diarrhea on all those people in the lake with me was beyond the pale of what I was willing to do, and my fellow swimmers might do more than just give me dirty looks. They might put me in an alligator death roll to hasten my demise.

I floated on my back the rest of the way and eventually made it to shore, where a team of strippers awaited me—not naked men or women who offer you a dance and a flirtatious compliment, but volunteers who throw you on the ground to strip your wetsuit off.

One young man grabbed me by the ankles and hiked me up like he was going to help me deliver a baby. He pulled at my wetsuit until it felt like my balls were going to pop off and fall on the ground. He pulled so hard, I began sliding across the tarmac like we were in some backwards Slip 'N Slide wheelbarrow race.

I got through that ordeal, and the only thing standing between me and relief was 874 yards to the transition tent, where a porta potty awaited. You make that run barefoot on pavement covered with slippery carpet through a chute where throngs of people on either side cheer you on to the 112-mile bike race.

I've been in that throng, cheering friends, and there is one thing I distinctly remember. As you watch the athletes run past, you can tell who is probably not going to finish the race. They have the same look Roberto Durán had in the eighth round in his fight against Sugar Ray Leonard, and you know they are one punch to the face away from throwing in the towel and mumbling, *"No más."* I knew I had that look. I was in bad shape.

I trudged to the tent and spent the next twenty minutes crouched over a pit filled with excrement in a 110-degree shit-sauna, crapping so violently I feared that my liver might be among the spray of brown putrid liquid shooting out of my ass. I wondered how on earth I was now going to bike 112 miles and then run a marathon—and why in hell I wanted to.

CHAPTER 2
ORIGIN STORY

Disturb us, Lord, when
We are too well pleased with ourselves,
When our dreams have come true
Because we have dreamed too little,
When we arrived safely
Because we sailed too close to the shore.
Disturb us, Lord, to dare more boldly,
To venture on wider seas
Where storms will show your mastery;
Where losing sight of land,
We shall find the stars.
— Sir Francis Drake

Why *did* I want to do Ironmans? What's wrong with golf? Golf's nice. You swing a club leisurely, hop in a little cart that takes you to your ball, and do it again. Then you go to the clubhouse and eat a hot dog and drink a beer. Not grueling in the least. Quite pleasant, actually.

You have to be stoned out of your mind to decide to do Ironman races. Like eating an entire bag of Doritos at 3 a.m.-stoned. Like drinking a bottle of vodka and calling your ex-girlfriend to see if there is still a spark-stoned.

Only a person whose good sense was severely impaired would decide to do a race marked by such agony and suffering that it made no sense to normal people. Normal people ponder whether Ironman is the design of al-Qaeda experimenting with torture techniques to inflict on Westerners.

Nope—just the result of a bunch of drunk, testosterone-fueled men trying to one-up each other.

It should be no surprise that the Ironman race was dreamed up by a U.S. Navy officer named John Collins during a beer-influenced debate over who the fittest athletes were: swimmers, cyclists, or runners. John Collins must have been full of Tom Collinses when he came up with the idea to help settle the issue.

I've reconstructed the likely conversation here:

Collins: "Let's come up with a race to find out who is the fittest athlete. We'll do the swim first."

Friend 1: "So we'll swim some laps in a lane in a heated pool, like at a swim meet?"

Collins: "No, you big sissy. We'll swim in a freezing, shark-infested ocean with waves and currents and the salt water blinding us and jellyfish stinging us. Plus, we'll have the threat of tropical storms to make it interesting."

Friend 2: "Will we each swim one at a time?"

Collins: "God no! Everyone will go at the same time so they can swim over each other, kick each other, pull each other, punch, claw, scratch, drown. It will be like the front row of a Who concert…but in the water."

Friend 1: "How far will we swim? A 100-meter freestyle?"

Collins: "Hell no! We'll swim two and a half miles so our lungs feel like they're going to explode and our legs become so tired we can barely walk on them when we get out. The threat of drowning should be a real factor."

Friend 2: "After we finish the swim, we change and eat and drink and rest, and then bike the next day?"

Collins: "You delicate flower! Fuck no! You take a crap, eat a donut, and get on the bike for a 112-mile ride under a scorching, heat-stroke-inducing sun. To get the heart pumping even more, hurricane-level winds will gust directly in your face for at least half the ride and threaten to blow you off the road for the other half."

Friend 1: "And would we do this over a period of two or three days?"

Collins: "Are you shitting me? You need to finish the bike in eight hours, or you're disqualified."

Friend 2: "And how many people are on the bike relay teams? Four?"

Collins: "Relay teams?? Seriously? Put away your pacifier, you big pussy. You'll bike the 112 miles by yourself until your ass is so raw from sitting on the saddle for seven hours that it will feel like someone beat you with a paddle, and your balls will be so numb you'll believe you'll never have children again."

Friend 1: "And then we're done? We'll have dinner, get a good night's sleep, and rise early for the run?"

Collins: "Hell no! I'll set aside a couple seconds for everyone to puke, and then you'll drink a couple bottles of Coke or a can of beer, eat a Big Mac, put on some running sneakers, and run."

Friend 2: "What are we running? A 10K or something? I imagine you'll want the race finished before it gets dark and runners can't see the road anymore."

Collins: "Come on, you undercooked cupcake! You'll run a full 26.2-mile marathon or as far as you can until your knees shatter, your organs fail, or you start hallucinating and have to be transported to a hospital where a doctor can hook you to an IV and a nurse can massage your leg muscles until they stop convulsing."

Friend 1: "After all of this, what do you get if you win? What's the prize money?"

Collins: "Seriously, you guys are beginning to annoy me. There is no prize money. People will lose money on this race, what with registration fees, hotels, flights, paying support crews, and meals. But the winner will get to call himself the Ironman."

Friend 2: "That's it?"

Collins: "That's it. So…are you in?"

Friend 1: "Damn right, I'm in!"

Friend 2: "Where do I sign up?"

———

For the record, Collins has maintained that this Ironman idea wasn't hatched by "a bunch of drunks in a Honolulu bar." He was at an awards ceremony for the Oahu Perimeter Relay running race, where he and some of his swim club buddies were debating who was in better shape, swimmers or runners (over beers, he admits. The defense rests).

Collins had just read a recent article in *Sports Illustrated* that declared that the great Belgian cyclist Eddy Merckx had the highest "oxygen uptake" (today known as VO_2 max or aerobic capacity) of any athlete ever recorded. So, he argued, cyclists should be included in the debate.

Collins devised a plan to combine the Waikiki Roughwater Swim with the Around Oahu Bike Race and the Honolulu Marathon. The next year, in the wee morning hours of February 18, 1978, in Oahu, Hawaii, the plan came to fruition, and the first Ironman was run.

Fifteen people lined up that day to compete. Collins's pre-race instructions to them included a handwritten note that said, "*Swim 2.4 miles! Bike 112 miles! Run 26.2 miles! Brag for the rest of your life.*"

Among the athletes: a guy who could barely tread water, let alone swim; a guy who bought a bicycle and learned to ride it the day before the race; a guy who took a mid-race break at

McDonald's; and a marine who had not ridden a bike since the fourth grade and got lost during the race.

The man who led the race most of the way was a twenty-five-year-old former Navy SEAL named John Dunbar, who had spent precious sleep hours the night before packing supplies. Apparently, he forgot to pack cycling shorts and had to borrow a pair after the swim. Legend has it that his support van got lost and that ten miles from the marathon finish, he ran out of drinking water and resorted to guzzling two cans of beer. He staggered to the finish line hallucinating and accusing his support-van driver of trying to poison him.

The winner was a former taxi driver and also a Navy man, a twenty-eight-year-old named Gordon Haller. Haller stumbled across the finish line after 11 hours, 46 minutes, and 58 seconds.

At the end of the long day, twelve of the fifteen participants crossed the finish line. That first Ironman seemed like a cosmic experiment, not only to the race organizer but also to each of the racers. And it gives me great comfort to know that these pioneers also did stupid things before and during their races.

~

My involvement in racing in general, and Ironman specifically, seems as accidental and experimental as those early athletes.

I began my racing career at the tender age of thirty-two with the 7.2-mile Falmouth Road Race in 2003 when the boyfriend of a girl I worked with and had a crush on twisted his ankle a week before the race. She was looking for someone to take his place and run with her.

I was not a runner. In fact, I hadn't run in any capacity for years. I was also in the middle of one of those fad diets of pizza, beer, and ice cream that I had picked up in college and had continued for the past ten years. But I was not going to let this very cute, very athletic young lady race alone.

I ran two practice runs totaling 3.4 miles and declared myself ready. Unfortunately, on race day, I learned that my office crush was also very fast. I kept up with her for five miles before my adrenaline ran out and my raging hormones couldn't overcome the pain anymore. I limped the final two miles and then couldn't walk the next two days.

Spending two days propped on the couch with ice bags covering my legs should have taught me a lesson for future races. It didn't. My next race was the Baltimore Marathon in 2010. The scenario was somewhat familiar: my friend Jim, who lives in Massachusetts, was running the Baltimore Marathon and wanted someone to run it with him. I lived in Washington, DC, at the time, so I was an obvious candidate.

At six feet, two inches, weighing about 240 pounds, and not being blessed with breasts—or at least the kind I was attracted to—Jim could not play the cute girl card that was such an effective motivation for getting me to race the Falmouth Road Race. But he was my friend, so I decided to join him. Maybe it would be fun.

Besides, I had just returned from Iraq, where I had spent all my non-working hours in the gym. I played basketball or soccer every night at the U.S. Embassy in Baghdad with the State Department staff and the Peruvian guards who protected the embassy. I was in the best shape of my life.

Thanks to my better fitness baseline—certainly not superior preparation—I fared better in Baltimore than in Falmouth. I clocked in at a respectable 4 hours and 2 minutes, and I only spent one day packed in ice this time.

Jim sucked me into another marathon in January 2011: the Walt Disney World Marathon. I chased Tinker Bell for two hours and paid for it by spending the rest of the day as the Tin Man, pre-oil can. I spent the night lying in bed, suffering, my legs wrapped in ice again.

Around this time, Jim said he had a new plan. I thought he might want to invest in an ice company. Instead, he decided the pain brought on by a marathon alone was not sufficient. As we approached our forties, we needed a more thorough way to inflict harm on our aging bodies. Or, more accurately, Jim saw a Facebook post by Providence College classmate Karen Pedlow stating that she was doing an Ironman.

Now, understand that Jim knew nothing about Ironman. He thought only professionals did Ironmans, and while Karen was athletic enough, he couldn't believe that she could be one of these mythical animals that could swim 2.4 miles, bike 112 miles, and then run a marathon.

We learned that you didn't have to be a pro to do an Ironman. Any moron could sign up and attempt it. All you had to do was take out a small loan to afford the registration fee, flights, accommodations, new bike, bike shipment, training costs, new wetsuit, massage therapist costs, and chiropractor visits. But we'd worry about all that later. We knew we had to try it.

Why didn't we start with a more bite-sized challenge, you ask? Why not a sprint, or Olympic tri, or even a Half Ironman first? Because Karen Pedlow did an Ironman, goddammit, and if she could do one, we could too.

And, frankly, because we are idiots. The last time I had swum laps was in 1976 at the YMCA in Lowell, Massachusetts, where I received a trophy for swimming one length of the pool. Jim didn't even have a road bike. He wasn't going to get very far riding his Huffy cruiser.

We began to research races and settled on Lake Placid, a vintage little village nestled in the Adirondack Mountains in upstate New York, home of the 1980 Winter Olympics and the site of the greatest sports upset in history: the U.S. hockey team's Miracle on Ice against the Soviets.

Besides the natural beauty and historic setting, we picked Lake Placid because my Uncle Bob had done it every year for the past ten years and said it was his favorite. He and my Aunt

Connie had the whole operation dialed in. They could give us guidance on not only the race itself, but also how to prepare in the days leading up to the race, where to stay, and all the peripheral concerns, like what activities to plan for family members while we racked our bikes and took practice laps in the lake.

The one thing we didn't count on was that registering for an Ironman was almost as challenging as racing one. They often sold out seconds after going on sale. Not surprisingly, when we tried to register for the 2011 race, it was already booked.

After some gnashing of teeth and a little more research, we learned that if you serve as a volunteer for a race, you're given preferential treatment for the next year's race. You are essentially guaranteed entry. A volunteer could do anything from helping register athletes to donning latex gloves to slather Vaseline all over their putrid nether regions in the transition tents. I asked Jim who we had to bribe so we didn't get stuck doing that.

We signed up as volunteers for the 2011 Ironman Lake Placid and soon discovered another acute challenge: finding accommodations. Every inn, hotel, motel, lodge, house, and room within fifteen miles was booked. Nearly all of them required a five- or seven-night minimum stay.

A house in town with a seven-night minimum started at $5,000, for example. A suite at the Golden Arrow Lakeside Resort near the beach where the swim started cost just under

$2,500 for a five-night stay. Other hotels and inns had similar rates, yet they all sold out a year in advance.

"So, Jim, where are we going to stay?" I asked a month before we were supposed to arrive for our volunteer duty.

"Don't worry. I've got you covered."

"What do you mean, 'I've got you covered'? Do we have a place?"

"I'm working on it."

"How much is it going to cost?"

"Cheap. Don't worry, Russ. I'm the man with the plan."

I'll spare you the suspense. He did have us covered— with a tent and a tarp. We pulled into North Pole Resorts in Wilmington, New York, which is ten miles outside of Lake Placid, where Jim had rented a campsite. He began putting up his tent. I wanted to complain—oh, how I wanted to complain—but he *had* found a place for us to stay under extremely challenging circumstances. And it was cheap.

Truth be told, a wave of nostalgia washed over me as I remembered childhood camping trips at Sebago Lake in Maine. The scent of pine trees and campfires. Roasting marshmallows and telling ghost stories.

I had my chance to complain that night when, twenty minutes into our slumber, the tent collapsed on one side. Then thirty seconds later, the other side collapsed. We scooched to the middle. Then it started raining. We were huddled in the middle of the tent, the roof three inches from our faces, rain leaking through, drip, drip, dripping on our heads. That might have been entertaining when I was seven years old, but not at forty. I ended up moving to the car and sleeping there. "You've got it covered alright," I grumbled.

TIP: Book your accommodations a year in advance and spend the money to rent a place close to the athletes' village and race locations. You want to be close to the action so that it is easy for you and your family if they come to watch you.

The next morning, we showed up waterlogged and bleary-eyed to The Pines Inn (five-night minimum stay at $189 per night!) to meet the volunteer coordinator for Ironman and get our assignments for race day.

The Pines Inn was emblematic of the rich history of Lake Placid as a tourist and winter sports mecca. The antique sleds, snowshoes, and skis adorning the knotty pine walls captured the nostalgia of an earlier age.

Opened in the summer of 1900, the inn once featured a house orchestra and dancing led by Miss Bessie Spectre of the New England Conservatory of Music. It

became a popular destination for the well-to-do, the famous...and bobsled groups.

In addition to Robert F. Kennedy, Vladimir Horowitz, and Albert Einstein, who summered in nearby Saranac Lake, the Italian bobsled team stayed there in 1960 and had such a good experience that the inn became the headquarters for the Italian and Swiss teams during the World Bobsled Championship in 1961.

Jill Cardinale, the cheerful owner of The Pines Inn and our volunteer coordinator, greeted us. "Good morning!! My name is Jill, and I'm so excited to have you assigned to my volunteer station! You have all signed up to be road marshals, right?"

I had no idea.

I turned to Jim. "Did we?"

"Yes, you dumbass. Didn't you read your emails? Jill sent us about twenty messages welcoming us and giving us instructions."

"I didn't see them. Is road marshal a good job?"

Jim shook his head. "Just shut up and listen. Moron."

Jill began to explain what being a road marshal entailed. "You have signed up to be a road marshal. This is a really important job." She said this with the earnestness of a school-teacher telling a kindergarten kid that washing his hands to kill germs was a really important job. "You are responsible for keeping the athletes and spectators safe during the bike course."

Jim and I were assigned the "hot corner": Main Street and Cummings Road, right in the center of Lake Placid. The famous Olympic Speed Skating Oval was at our backs below, and the Miracle on Ice hockey arena loomed above us to our left. We were stationed at the bottom of a steep hill. Riders would come screaming down the hill and then have to negotiate the sharp turn onto Cummings.

So our first job during the five-hour shift was to give the cyclists a slow-down signal so they wouldn't miss the turn and careen into a crowd of spectators.

Our other job was to let people cross the road when there was a gap between riders. The fact that they trusted two bird-brains with the safety of cyclists and spectators made me question whether these people at Lake Placid Ironman really knew what they were doing. Odds were good that we'd time a gap wrong and kill a rider or get some poor tourist horribly maimed.

"I know you will all enjoy this assignment," Jill concluded. "It's a perfect location, and the timing is great, so you can watch the start and finish of the race and volunteer in the middle of the day! Keep everyone safe out there."

The next morning, having successfully not gotten anyone maimed, Jim and I woke up at 3 a.m. and continued our camping adventure—this time in a line that snaked a quarter mile outside the Lake Placid High School. Hundreds of volunteers huddled in the cold for hours to ensure that they'd be able to register for the 2012 race before it sold out.

We finally made it inside and paid our $750 fee. We each got a confirmation card and waved it around like we were one of the kids who won a golden ticket in *Charlie and the Chocolate Factory*. Then we looked at each other and said, "What the fuck did we just get ourselves into?"

CHAPTER 3

TRANSITION

Life is pleasant. Death is peaceful.
It's the transition that's troublesome.

— Isaac Asimov

As I crouched over the porta potty toilet (you don't sit on the seat unless you want to catch giardia or some similarly pleasant parasitic infection), I pondered whether to go on. I was exhausted. Whether that was because I had swum 2.4 miles with the sangfroid of the Titanic after the iceberg, or because I had just spent twenty minutes imitating the Niagara Falls, I wasn't entirely sure.

I mustered the strength to stumble into the T1, or the first transition tent. This is where athletes change into their bike gear, grab a tube of gel or a ham sandwich and some water or Gatorade. A pro will spend less than two and a half minutes in that tent. Patrick Lange, winner of the 2018 Ironman World Championship in Kona, Hawaii, transitioned from swim to bike in two minutes and five seconds.

I seem to spend more time transitioning *to* the bike than it takes Patrick Lange to ride the 112 miles *on* the bike. This baffles Jim. "What the hell do you do in there? Was there a buffet table I missed? Did you watch a matinee of *Breaking Away*?"

The truth is, I don't know what took me so long in transition. I moved as fast as I could. It's not like I wanted to spend any more time there than I had to. The transition tent after the swim is essentially the nastiest Turkish bath house you can imagine. It's a toddler shit explosion. A toxic waste dump. A decomposing rat hovel. Wading through a putrid septic tank would be pleasant in comparison.

Guys smelling like the New Jersey Turnpike married the Boston Bruins locker room walk around with their junk hanging out. God bless the volunteers who get stuck with transition tent duty and enthusiastically help you pull your bike shorts on, rub sunscreen on your arms and legs, take your swampy wetsuit from you, and send you on your way. Mike Rowe of *Dirty Jobs* would say, "Fuck that. I'm not going near there."

And T1 is nice compared to the transition from bike to run, or T2. For T2, add the equivalent of 2500 diarrhea-filled diapers and 1000 vomit-scented candles to T1.

As I sat eating my peanut butter, jelly, chia seed, and cinnamon on Wonder Bread sandwich, I recalled Jim's T2 experience during that first race in Lake Placid in 2012. "I should have been pulled off the race after the bike," he said later that night. "I got into the transition tent, and my pee was black. Then I started running, and I couldn't run straight. I started running sideways."

He must have looked like one of those intrepid newscasters reporting a hurricane who cling desperately to a street pole until they get blown sideways down the street. Jim was certain a volunteer or race official would notice that he was moving as if he was running through a tornado and pull him off the race.

I had the same thought now. I must have looked sea-green seasick. Surely someone would pull me aside and say, "Buddy, you don't look so good. I don't think it's such a good idea for you to continue the race."

I finished my sandwich, slugged down a Nuun electrolyte drink, took a piss, and sat down for a moment. My stomach still felt queasy, but I decided I'd start the ride and see if it improved.

TIP: Rain can happen. The night before the race, put a Solo cup over your transition bag. Poke a hole in it and pull the bag drawstring through the hole. Also, put a bag over your bike seat in case it rains. Get to the race site 75–80 minutes early so you have time to fix or adjust things.

I walked my bike out of transition, clipped into the pedals, and prepared my mind for the equivalent of cycling from New York City to Philadelphia and then tacking on another twenty-mile ride for the hell of it. One hundred and twelve miles...*by bike.* I knew if I didn't start feeling better soon, I wasn't going to make it.

CHAPTER 4

LANCE WAS WRONG— IT *IS* ABOUT THE BIKE

Nothing compares to the simple pleasure of a bike ride.
— John F. Kennedy

Miles 1–3 (bike), 2.4–5.4 (total race miles):

TIP: Let some air out of your bike tires the day before the race so they don't pop overnight. You can pump them up in the morning. Some race mornings at the bike setup have sounded like someone was popping popcorn, and the last thing you need when you get to your bike is to have to replace a burst tube.

The Lake Placid bike course starts with a steep downhill through town, from School Street to Colden Avenue. I took a deep breath, let the cool morning air wash over me, and coasted through the neighborhood streets lined with cheering people. They were cheering for me not to die. At the base of Colden, there is a sharp left turn, where volunteers give riders the "slow down!" signal.

It would be entirely possible to go too fast, miss the turn, crash into spectators, and end your bike race before you rode 200 yards. I am stupid enough to do that on most days, but not today. I wasn't racing yet. I was trying to survive.

TIP: Take Claritin before the swim. Otherwise you'll waste energy blowing snot rockets the whole bike ride. And the other riders around you won't appreciate you blowing your nose on them.

The first few miles on the bike of any Ironman race are a settling-in, feeling-out period. (Conversely, the last few miles are when you're trying to get back feeling in your feet and legs.) There are days when you hop on the bike and feel fast—when you're strong and the wind is at your back and you're flying as if you're riding on a long downhill. And there are days when you feel like you're riding a tricycle in sand.

For example, I knew within the first three miles of the bike in Ironman Boulder in 2014 that it was going to be a rough day. You either have it or you don't. At Boulder, I didn't. I was fatigued early, and to this day, Ironman Boulder is my worst finish. Worse still, that rat-bastard, Jim, beat me.

I had hoped to test my prowess against Jim in this race, but he decided to do Ironman Chattanooga instead. I guess he got tired of me beating him in Lake Placid.

As I pedaled through the residential neighborhoods of Lake Placid before turning onto Route 73, I had the same feeling I had had at Boulder. I settled into the seat and prepared for a long, difficult day.

I huffed and puffed past Lisa G's, Lamb Lumber Company, Schulte's Family Lodge, and the Carriage House Motor Inn. Then, a half a mile up ahead to the right, I spied two towers jutting out over the trees like concrete mountain peaks—the Olympic ski jumps. You can see them from most locations in Lake Placid. They poke the sky over the town just as the two twin towers of the World Trade Center once loomed over New York City.

Jim, Mark, and I had gone up there earlier in the week. We rode the elevator to the top of the jump and contemplated what it would be like to launch down the slope and fly in the air more than the length of a football field.

Television doesn't do justice to the incredible height of the jumps. Nor does looking up at them from below. Only when you're standing at the top, 120 meters high and nearly a hundred feet higher than the Statue of Liberty, do you grasp the insanity of launching yourself down it.

I pressed on and came to the Lake Placid Horse Shows and Equestrian Stadium. This is where the Opening Ceremony for the 1980 Games was held. Ironman Lake Placid once hosted a pasta dinner here the night before the race. Though not on the scale of an Olympic opening ceremony, it may have been as inspiring.

I attended in 2012, and hundreds of athletes and their families gathered for rigatoni and to hear heartfelt speeches about perseverance and overcoming adversity. They also showed a film that highlighted different athletes' journeys to get to this point. Cancer survivors, recent heart attack victims, amputees. The oldest and youngest participants (a seventy-eight-year-old man and an eighteen-year-old young woman who would feel like a seventy-eight-year-old man after the race) were called to the stage and interviewed.

It was intimidating seeing hundreds of Greek gods carved by hours of exercise. Everyone was sizing everyone else up. That happened all weekend. You'd walk by a guy who might have the slightest paunch or a woman who was slight and think, Well, I'll certainly beat them. Then, later in the race, the guy with the gut would blow by you on the bike, and the woman would cruise past you on the run.

This "opening ceremony" was two hundred lions strutting around, assessing who was the alpha that would lead the pride. It was a group of peacocks puffing their plumes. It was a Miss America swimsuit competition. "Geez, I'm feeling a little inadequate with all these chiseled people around me. They all brought six-packs, and I brought a keg," Jim said, holding his belly.

"How do you think I feel?" his wife Melissa answered.

Miles 3–5 (5.4–7.4)

I wished they hadn't discontinued that dinner. It was a special evening and made you proud to be participating in the race. All of a sudden, I found myself climbing a series of hills that rise around 500 feet for the next five miles. They are called the Jackrabbit Rollers.

I slogged up the elevations, exerting a tremendous amount of energy on every pedal stroke just to inch forward. It felt like my tires were flat. They weren't. My legs were dead from the swim. Today was just going to be a dead-legs, tricycle-in-the-sand type of day.

It's not surprising that the first section of the Lake Placid bike course includes a few long climbs. It is in the Adirondack Mountains after all. While the Adirondacks will never be confused with the Himalayas, the bike course is still considered one of the toughest—if not the toughest—in the Ironman circuit. There is 4,182 feet of elevation gain, a not-insignificant amount. It can still crush your soul like Tom Brady driving at the end of the fourth quarter against your team to win another Super Bowl.

TIP: If people are hammering up the hills and passing you during the first five to ten miles of a race, let them. Take it easy at the start. Let them pass you. They're practicing irrational exuberance, and you'll pass 95 percent of them on the second loop because their legs are shot. 'It's a marathon, not a sprint' is a well-worn cliché for a reason.

Like my swim, I had high hopes for a great bike ride. I had never had a good bike ride in an Ironman, and this time, I wanted one worse than Jim wants a cheesesteak sub three meals a day. I thought I had prepared well.

For the past two months, I had been biking the twenty miles to work from Reston, Virginia, to my communications job at the Department of Interior in Washington, DC (we had moved back East from California the previous year to be closer to family). Forty miles a day, four or five days a week. The Old Dominion bike trail on which I rode was flush with other cycling commuters, and I was racing them all.

"Jim, these other commuters may be fooling others about their intentions, but they're not fooling me. When guys are rolling up in high-end cycling shorts and aerodynamic team jerseys, clipped into Speedplay pedals with Zipp wheels on their $5,000 Treks, they're racing, whether they admit it or not. And the three words these guys hate to hear are 'on your left.' That means I'm passing their asses."

"Why do you turn into little Napoleon in sports?" Jim said.

I was always the smallest kid in my class at school growing up—which meant I was always the smallest kid on the soccer field, basketball team, tennis court, hockey rink, and so on. I loved playing sports, but because of my lack of size and strength, when people were picking teams, I always got picked last.

Consequently, I developed a chip on my shoulder the size of George Washington's forehead on Mount Rushmore. To make up for my Lilliputian stature and to show those guys who overlooked me, I fought for every inch as if my life depended on it. I was the scrappy guy who never made an all-star team but won the hustle award every year and got into a fight every game.

This is a long way of saying that, for reasons related to nature, I was one of those guys on the bike. I HATED getting passed. Something about a guy shouting "On your left" and whizzing by turns me into Pete Rose on two wheels.

At the beginning of the two months, I was getting passed a lot. One morning, an older guy passed me. I say older, but he was probably my age. I often forget that I am no longer a young guy. I tried to stay with him, and I did so for about seven miles. Then he dumped me. I just couldn't keep his pace, and I was ticked. I vowed that when I got within a month of Ironman Lake Placid, nobody would pass me.

"Jim, just like I told you. Now I'm doing the dropping. I'm the fucking American Sniper, just picking off other cyclists one after the other. Pfft. Pfft. Pfft. Dusted. I'm not getting passed on the Old Dominion Trail again. Ever. I'll bike myself into asphyxiation before I'll let someone pass me. Pfft! Pfft!" And I didn't.

One woman, sitting jauntily on her seat, breezed by me one day, looking like it took no effort at all. I checked my speedometer. I was doing 25 mph, and working hard to do it, thank you very much. I was pissed. I began to pick up my pace, gasping for breath. She tra la la'd along and increased the gap.

Was she some sort of superhero? Was there an Avenger whose superpower was riding bikes superfast with no effort? I cranked it up as fast as I could go. Then I figured it out. I spied the little box near her pedals. E-bike. She was riding an electric bike, meaning she was riding a Vespa with pedals. All right. I was still the American Sniper of the Old Dominion bike trail.

I thought I was going to continue to be the American Sniper at Lake Placid. In addition to my triumph on the Old Dominion commuter circuit, for the first time I finally had all the right equipment. I had raced this course twice before. I knew what I was up against and what I had to do. At least this time I'd be riding my own bike.

In 2012, I didn't have a clue. A month before the race, I decided that my Scattante R660 road bike wasn't worth paying $300 to ship across the country from California to Lake Placid. I'd rent a bike onsite instead.

"You're what?" Jim said. "You're going to rent a bike that you've never ridden to do your first Ironman? You're insane." I didn't know what I didn't know.

Hell, I'd been training on my buddy's twelve-year-old son's beat up, rusted Trek mountain bike for much of the spring because the Scattante was stuck in Washington, DC. I had moved to California in January of 2012 to start the new job as a writer for Disney. Karoline had stayed behind to pack up our DC condo and ship everything west.

I should point out that at this time, we had no kids. And since Karoline was in DC until March, I had nearly three months on my own. Endless hours to train. Oh, how I squandered those sacred training opportunities by puttering around Rodeo Drive on a kid's wobbly dirt bike.

My bike didn't get to California until June. While it was an improvement over the rusted Trek, it still wasn't very good, and I didn't want to attempt my first Ironman on it.

Of course, with only a month until the race, all the bike shops in the Lake Placid area were sold out. I wasn't sure where I was going to find a bike and started calling shops in Massachusetts, near where Jim lived.

"Jim, I don't know what I'm going to do," I said. "There's not a single bike for rent within fifty miles. This is a disaster."

"I told you this would happen," Jim said, "but do you listen to me? No."

"What am I going to do if I can't find a bike?"

"Maybe you could borrow a horse," he said.

Then Brian Delaney, the owner of High Peaks Cyclery in Lake Placid, called.

"How tall are you?" he asked. When I told him that I was five foot six, he told me I could rent his wife's Serrota Nove for $300. I had never heard of that brand. I looked it up on the internet and read a few write-ups. *Accelerates swiftly, handles like a sports car, comfortably efficient—a bike with epic capabilities!!*

Epic capabilities for an epic race! Sold! Brian assured me it was a great bike and would do just fine in the race. Two days before the Ironman, I walked into his shop, did a quick fitting, took the Serrota for a short spin, and deemed it comfortably efficient enough.

I'm certain I was the only person riding a Serrota Nove that day. The most popular bike by far in Ironman races is Cervelo, followed by Trek and Specialized. But you'd have to search far and wide on the Ironman circuit to find a Serrota.

The other thing I learned is that there are road bikes and triathlon, or tri, bikes. The Serrota was a road bike. It is hard to tell any difference between the two looking with an untrained eye. The main difference is the geometry of the frame.

A tri bike is built with a steeper, more aggressive seat tube angle than that of a road bike, which puts the rider into a forward lean that allows him to ride in a much more aerodynamic position. This angle also places the rider's hips over the crankset, which engages his quadriceps more for increased power.

The bottom line is tri bikes are designed to help riders ride faster than road bikes. The drawback is being in that position for five or six hours can be miserable. Giving an NFL offensive lineman a piggyback ride through the Grand Canyon might be less excruciating.

Most people find road bikes to be much more comfortable over long distances. You have more options to sit up and give your back a break. You can place your hands in multiple positions on the handlebars.

"My only regret is this is a road bike and not a tri bike," I said. "I won't be able to get into aero position and be as streamlined as I'd like."

"Who are you trying to kid?" Jim said. "Two hours ago, you didn't know a road bike from a skateboard. Now you're worried about being more aero. Try being me. My closest bike comp is a refrigerator on a dolly."

I also didn't know at the time that moving the seat up or down or the handlebars forward as much as a centimeter could mean the difference between comfort and multiple chiropractor visits.

"You're nuts," Uncle Bob said. "Nobody in their right mind would ride a bike they've never ridden for their first Ironman." He inspected the bike. "Do you have a bento box?"

"What's that?" I asked.

"It's a bag that goes across your crossbar where you put your snacks and salt tabs and stuff."

"No, I don't."

"Go buy one. They sell them at the athletes' village. They're about twenty bucks."

"I'll just cut a water bottle in half and tape it to the bar," I said. "I'm trying to limit my spending."

Uncle Bob just shook his head. "You're $10,000 in, and now you're trying to cut costs? You're unbelievable. How about CO_2 cartridges? Do you have those?"

"What are those for?"

"They're in case you get a flat. Do you have spare tubes?"

I didn't have anything. I asked Jim what he had packed for the bike. He pulled out a pre-race packing list that his coach at Endurance Nation had given him. The list included bicycle, helmet, bike shoes, bike pump, nutritional supplies, salt tabs, bento box, one spare tire, four spare tubes, four CO_2 cartridges, chain degreaser, chain lube, a rag, and a complete bike tool kit (tire levers, an Allen wrench set, and a patch kit).

The only things I had from that list were the bike, helmet, and shoes, and I barely had the bike. My helmet was a cheap child's helmet with a dent in the front of it from when I flipped over my handlebars and landed on my face a few months prior to the race.

My shoes were also a cheap pair and too loose on my feet. If I wore a Hefty trash bag for a shirt and cut-off jeans for shorts, it wouldn't have surprised anyone. Despite all this, I finished the bike that first race in 6 hours and 50 minutes. Not great but, considering the circumstances, as well as I could have expected.

This race, I expected more.

After renting a bike for my first Ironman, and then carrying on a brief affair with a Trek road bike that was too big for me for my second one, I finally bought the brand that was ubiquitous at Ironman events: Cervelo. I went with a moderately priced ($1,959.99) 2015 P2 tri bike, the low end of Cervelo's triathlon series. Screw comfort! I wanted speed.

I then took the bike to Incycle Bicycles in Pasadena for a professional bike fit. The shop's motto—*Incycle Bicycles believes in harnessing the power of bikes to advance the good in us all*—seemed incongruous to my goals. I didn't care about advancing the good in me. I wanted to harness the power of my bike to kick Jim's ass.

TIP: Get a professional bike fit. And get a bike that fits. Riding an Ironman on a bike that is two sizes too big for you, or new to you, is like trying to run a marathon in a pair of six-inch heels.

Each year and each race featured an equipment improvement. One year, I swapped out my $40 child helmet for a $200 super lightweight Kask Mojito 16 helmet, which was much more aerodynamic than my dinged old one.

Another year, it was new Bont Riot TR+ bike shoes, which were known for having exceptional fit and comfort. Bont is a small Australian company out of Sydney with a long history of making ice skates. Their expertise in molding full-carbon skates that maximized efficiency and power translated well to the bike shoe market, where heat-molded carbon shoes give a rider excellent power transfer to the pedals.

My old shoes, with cheap injection-molded plastic soles, were heavier and more prone to flexing. The Bont Riots, with heat-molded carbon soles, were stiff, meaning more power transfer…meaning faster.

The next evolution in bike gear was to upgrade my race jersey and bike pants. I went with the $120 Sportful Bodyfit Pro Race Jersey and $180 Pro LTD Bib Short. This pair was featured in *Triathlete Magazine*'s 2018 Buyer's Guide.

Here's the write up:

This is a serious kit for the serious cyclist. I'm a serious cyclist! I'm an American Sniper!!

Both pieces are spec'd out to be fast, with a wind-cheating design and proprietary performance fabrics. Fast!! Cheating!! I'm not above cheating to beat Jim. Besides, it's not cheating if you don't get caught!!!

Bonus: You'll feel like a Marvel hero in this kit.[1] As long as it's one who is fast – like Ironman!!

Then, the pièce de résistance. Just a few days before this current race, my buddy Mark, who along with Jim and another buddy, Jeff, were acting as my race Sherpas, let me borrow his Church carbon aero wheels. The serious cyclists (and I'm a serious cyclist!) use carbon aero wheels.

Jim and Mark swore that aero wheels, which have deeper rims that act like a sail when you pick up speed, would shave

---

1   Julia Beeson Polloreno, "Sportful Bodyfit," *Triathlete Magazine*, Spring 2018 Buyer's Guide.

time. They must be right, I reasoned, since all the pros rode aero wheels. Zipp is the most popular brand. A set of Zipp wheels costs twice as much as I spent on my entire bike. I couldn't yet justify to Karoline spending $4,000 on bike wheels.

I had never ridden aero wheels and peppered Mark and Jim with questions.

"Do they really work?" I asked Mark, an engineer. "Do they make a difference?"

"Absolutely," he said. "You'll definitely feel it, and once you get past 18 mph, you'll go faster with less effort. I guarantee it."

Faster with less effort was a no-brainer. "Sounds good to me," I said. "Can I use yours for the race?"

Mark hesitated. "You might want to try them first. They take some getting used to."

"What do you mean?" I asked.

"Because of the depth of the rim, aero wheels catch more wind. The best way to describe it is to think of wind filling a sail and propelling a sailboat forward. Same idea. If there is a cross wind, you'll feel it, and strong wind will blow you right off the road if you're not strong enough to power through it. Especially someone lighter like you, you want to be careful."

"Will they make me faster?"

"Definitely."

"Then let's do it. Take my slow wheels off and put your fast ones on my bike."

Here I was—again—adding an unknown element right before a grueling race, when normal people plot out every detail for months and then don't waiver from their well-conceived plans. Hot pepper shots, rented bikes, new wheels—when was I going to learn?

My new wheels made me a cocky bastard the night before the race. All of these upgrades in equipment and aerodynamic improvements would help me slay on the bike. I would finally finish an Ironman bike leg in under six hours. Heck, I might even toy with five hours. Pfft.

Instead, my bike picked up where my swim left off. Instead of being the American Sniper, I was AWOL. In the military, that generally means you are not where you are supposed to be at a particular time. I was supposed to be on the bike, riding the Jackrabbit Rollers.

Instead, I was crouched over a hole filled with shit, sweating profusely and clearing the system. Little did I know that this would be the least of my concerns that ride.

CHAPTER 5
TRAINING WITH KIDS

The pessimist complains about the wind; the optimist
expects it to change; the realist adjusts the sails.
— William Ward

Training for an Ironman with three kids under five compared to training with no kids is like watching a bad sitcom on network television versus HBO. The quality of the training, like the network sitcom, is cubic zirconia with large inclusions.

Like the network sitcom, you'll get interrupted every ten minutes with commercial breaks. But the ads aren't funny Bud Light ads. They are a shout from the bathroom from your three-year-old asking you to wipe his bum. Dilly, dilly, Daddy.

It never fails. The minute I hop on the stationary bike, Peter will ask for a glass of milk or some snack, Fintan will need help going potty, and Nora will walk up to the spinning wheel with the goal of seeing what happens when she sticks her finger in it.

Feed Peter. Wipe Fintan. Move Nora. Get back on the bike. A minute later:

"Dad, can you put on a movie for me?"

Or:

(Through tears:) "Daddy, I can't find my Spiderman guy."

Or:

(Through tears:) "Peter hit me!"

Or:

"I want pickles and fish for a snack." (Is my three-year-old pregnant?)

Or:

"Dada, goo goo gaa gaa, I'm going to stick my finger in your bike wheel again."

After fifteen minutes, I give up, grateful that I even got on a bike that day.

Where's my wife to help handle this barrage of requests? Being selfish again and cooking dinner in peace and quiet or putting away laundry, uninterrupted. Must be nice.

At the end of it all, nobody will be satisfied with the result, the ratings will tank, and I won't be renewed for another season. And, to top it off, I have to censor my language, so I can't even swear when I'm angry.

In the meantime, my kid-free friends, or friends with older, self-sufficient children, are at liberty to plan a lavish *Game of Thrones*-like, commercial-free production. They are uninterrupted, not hindered at all by the constraints of time or schedule, and can have the highest quality, most focused, and lavish concentration of training time in the history of mankind.

When we signed up to do Lake Placid in 2016, Jim hired a triathlon coach and shared his training schedule with me. A typical entry looked like this: Monday—6:30 a.m. Masters swim followed by an eight-mile run. Tuesday—ride outside for eighty miles and run one hour after. Wednesday—6:30 a.m. Masters swim, followed by strength training, followed by a twelve-mile run. And these were weekdays during which he worked a full-time job!

My training schedule looked like this: boys beat the crap out of me for eight hours, then I fall asleep on the couch, drool dripping down my chin. Fintan liked to slap me and tackle me to the ground. "Daddy, I'm going to punch you in the face and kill you…poop head!"

Peter liked to launch himself from the couch and jump on my back. "You are evil, and you smell, so I must destroy you!"

If I was training for WWE, I'd have the perfect children. But I wasn't. I was training for an Ironman, and I needed to see a chiropractor once a week to fix my back and a psychiatrist to fix my self-esteem. There were no eighty-mile bike rides followed by an hour run on my schedule.

TIP: Buy a BOB Rambler jogging stroller, with twelve-inch air-filled tires and "mountain bike style suspension system [for] an ultra-smooth ride."[1] Then, when you get multiple kids under five,

---

1   "BOB Rambler Jogging Stroller, Black [Old Version]," Amazon, https://www.amazon.com/BOB-Rambler-Jogging-Stroller-Black/dp/B074MF4M4Q.

upgrade to a double jogging stroller. Then buy a Burley D'Lite child bike trailer. This way, you can push your kids around on two-hour runs and haul them along on four-hour bike rides, while giving your spouse that kid-free alone time they crave. Training and precious family time, all in one!

The hardest part about training with kids, however, is not finding time; it's trying to fend off every disease they bring home from day care and school. Getting sick a few months ahead of the race is one thing. It sets your training back, but you have time to recover. But getting sick the week of a race is a disaster.

This is an acute problem for me because the bargain I've made with Karoline is to just give me two months before the race. If I want to stay married, I can't ask for six months or a year of intensive training time—what it takes to properly prepare for an Ironman. So I just maintain a base level of fitness for ten months and ask for the two months before the race. She grudgingly agrees to that.

When everyone is tapering—winding down their grueling schedule so they don't injure themselves or burn themselves out—I'm ramping up. The result is my body is exhausted, and my immune system is vulnerable. The two weeks leading up to an Ironman, I spend more money on Zicam and Airborne than on my running shoes. Sometimes, it's not enough.

The week of the Eagleman Half Ironman, which was held on the Eastern Shore of Maryland in June of 2018—a tune-up race for Lake Placid the following month—my throat felt like a baby bird was inside pecking at it.

Of course, whatever I had, I caught from my three kids, who were all sick. Three kids, three perpetual petri dishes. Every parent knows that one of the side effects of having kids in day care or school is they get sick all the time. I can guarantee only one direct result of my children's attendance at either institution, and it's not that they're learning things. It's that they get sick. Often.

Peter was a snot machine. Snot was flying everywhere. Mostly on me. Sneeze, snot shoots out, he eats it. Repeat every five minutes. As for Fintan, he was all stuffed up and didn't know quite how to blow his nose to get the boogies out. "I have boogies!!" he cried throughout the night. And he was coughing constantly. Nora too. Boogies, coughing, crying.

It's always worse at night. Restful sleep with babies and toddlers is an exercise in futility in and of itself, but sickness makes it an audacious goal to be achieved, not a standard operating procedure to be blissfully enjoyed.

The Monday night before the race went like this: when Karoline and I tried to put Nora to bed, she screamed as if I was jabbing her with a white-hot cattle prod. After two hours of that joyful bonding, she finally fell asleep. As did we. My slumber was short-lived, as Fintan began crying a mere fifteen minutes into it. He wanted his bottle, which is a sippy cup with PediaSure. I got him his bottle, gave him his baba (pacifier), and lay with him until he fell asleep. Then I returned to my bed.

I pulled the warm covers over and burrowed under the blankets to try to get some much-needed recovery rest, the bird continuing to peck, peck, peck away at my swollen tonsils. "Daddy, will you snuggle me?" Peter, the five-year-old, appeared before my bed like an apparition. The ghost of carnal sins past. I hadn't been in bed for thirty seconds. He snuck up like a goddamn black ops special forces soldier skulking into an enemy camp.

"No, Peter, I'm tired. Go back to bed."

"But I'm scared!"

"Scared of what?"

"Witches."

I got in bed with him, closed my eyes to prepare to sleep, and he posed a question.

"Daddy, what does hypnotize mean?"

"What?"

"What does hypnotize mean?"

"Where did you hear about this word? And why on God's earth are you asking it randomly at 2:07 a.m.?"

I told him it is like a magician doing a magic trick or when someone casts a spell on you and makes you do things you don't know you're doing. Goddammit!! I forgot about the witches! Now he'll be scared that a witch is going to hypnotize him. I'll never get to sleep.

Why do five-year-olds save all their questions of the day for precisely the time when all you want to do is sleep? God forbid I try to ask a question or talk to Peter if he's playing with his Legos or watching *Star Wars*. So now we went through various questions related to hypnotism and then moved on to the breezy topic of what happens to you when you die. *You may find out in a minute if you don't stop asking questions.*

Silence for a few moments. Then, "Dad, is there a Home Depot in heaven?"

Peter finally fell asleep, and I managed to get back to my bed for all of thirty minutes before Fintan showed up and begged me to come snuggle with him. I got out of the bed to escort him back to his room. "Uppies!" he said, arms outstretched for me to pick him up and carry him.

I picked him up, and he was soaking wet. He had peed himself. And, I'd soon discover, his bed. "Come on, I said, let's sleep in Mommy and Daddy's bed." That bed was already crowded with Nora and Karoline. Fintan complained that he wanted to be next to Mommy. Nora was nursing, so that was an impossibility that he didn't quite grasp.

He cried for a few minutes about wanting to be next to Mommy before I convinced him to snuggle with Daddy. Of course, with crying comes snots. "I have boogies!! I need a towel!" This went on for about fifteen minutes before he fell asleep again.

Ten minutes later, Peter the Apparition showed up at the side of my bed. "No fair!" he cried. "I want to come in too."

"Oh, dear Lord, get in then." I reached over to my iPhone and turned off the alarm set for 5 a.m. Screw the sixty-mile training ride I had scheduled. I needed sleep more than a bike ride.

Then this happened the very next night: Fintan came in the room at 4 a.m. "Snuggles," he said, as he reached out his arms. This meant he wanted me to bring him back to his bed and sleep with him there. The routine is I lie down with him for a few minutes, he falls asleep, and I go back to my bed.

This time was different. He was coughing—hacking. This was especially fun when he pulled my face close to his. I thought he was about to give me a kiss. So cute—a special 4 a.m. moment you cherish as a parent. No. He didn't kiss me. He coughed right into my mouth. And he did this for the next three hours.

The topper came at 7 a.m. when he announced that he was throwing up. Then he did. On me. I felt him. He was warm. He had a fever of 101.7 degrees. There went the mile swim at the YMCA I had planned that morning. I'd just have get in that final swim the day before the race—a little one-hundred-yard practice run to test the conditions and make sure my wetsuit wasn't ripped from when Peter tried to use it as a *Star Wars* costume.

That swim never happened due to another mistake I made.

I resorted to my old ruse that this would be a family vacation with a short race thrown in. I had booked a room for two nights at the Hyatt Regency Chesapeake Bay Golf Resort, Spa and Marina for the race-discounted rate of $746.84. Christmas would be light that year, but by golly, we'd have this family memory forever. "Look, honey, you can book a spa!"

Hopped up on Nuun immunity, Airborne, Cold-EEZE, Zicam, vitamin C, multivitamins, and chicken soup, I packed up the car on the Friday before the race, and the kids and I coughed and sneezed and sniffled the entire three-hour drive to the Hyatt.

I gamely pointed out amenities and activities that I had pre-selected as ones that might excite Karoline and the kids. Pools and a waterslide! Mini golf! Camp Hyatt at Pirate's Cove! An arcade and game room! Horseback rides! A corn maze! Horn Point Laboratory with a ninety-minute guided tour where the kids can learn about coastal resilience!!!

"That does all sound fun, honey," Karoline allowed. "I wouldn't mind trying some of those things—well, aside from the coastal resilience tour."

"Oh, I won't be able to join you, sweetie. I have to register and check in my bike and pick up some supplies at the athletes' village. I also want to put on my wetsuit and do a practice swim in the bay to get familiar with it. I was just trying to find things to do for you and the kids while I was getting all this other stuff out of the way."

"So you want me to cart three kids—one, you'll recall, that is only six months old—around this resort and the Eastern Shore by myself while you do your Ironman stuff all day?" She was just getting started.

"And then on Sunday, while you're out having a nice bike ride and run for six hours, I'll be hauling the same three kids through crowds of 10,000 people, trying to pack them up and find lunch and keep them from running through these muddy fields? Have you met your two-year-old? He loves to run away. Thinks it's a fun game. Is that what you envision? Me leaving our five-year-old to watch the baby while I chase Fintan through throngs of strange people?"

This conversation did not go how I planned it in my head, and I learned a valuable lesson: if you want to bring your family of two boisterous boys and a baby to your Ironman, don't…unless you have Sherpas to either take care of them or take care of you.

If you have ever watched National Geographic or Discovery, or read Jon Krakauer, you are familiar with the term Sherpa. Sherpas are locals of the Himalayan Mountains renowned for their skill in mountaineering. Expeditions attempting to climb Mount Everest employ Sherpas to guide them to the summits of the world's tallest mountains. For climbers attempting to summit Everest, Sherpas do everything from cook the meals to carry the oxygen to climb ahead and set the ropes.

In Ironman, Sherpa duties are usually taken on by a family member or friend, and they are every bit as essential to athletes trying to summit the Ironman course. They carry all your gear around for you. They retrieve your bike while you are doing the run and bring it back to the hotel or Airbnb. They push the baby stroller or carry the toddler on their shoulders through the crowds if you've brought your children. They keep you loose and calm in the days leading up to the race. They get you a beer after the race when you can't get up from the couch because your legs hurt too much.

I didn't bring a Sherpa to Maryland. I brought my wife, my five-year-old, two-year-old, and six-month-old. Five-year-olds and wives carrying two-year-olds and six-month-olds do not generally make good Sherpas.

Granted, it's a groovy experience for kids to get excited about a race and see their mom or dad cross the finish line and get a medal. But it's a grind for the spouse who has to cart them through crowds and schlep them all around for up to seventeen hours, all while worrying if you're going to drown, crash your bike, or have a heart attack during the run.

A wiser move would have been to bring a grandparent, friend, sibling, nanny, or local street urchin to help navigate the day. But I'm not wise.

Instead of swimming in the pools or playing at Pirate's Cove or touring the Horn Point Laboratory, the family spent all of Saturday morning waiting in long lines to fill out paper-work—such as the waiver that said if I died I would not hold the organizers responsible. Then we waited in other lines to get my race bib, timing chip, stickers for my bike, and other assorted instructions and swag—the highlight of which is a backpack that you get at every Ironman.

"Look how cool this backpack is," I said to Karoline, try-ing to show that the two hours we had spent waiting in line was now worth it.

She was probably thinking, *Gee, that's great. Only cost you one thousand dollars. I hope your race doesn't take as long as it did to get that stupid backpack.*

At this point, I should have read the room better. But I didn't. After tagging my bike and prepping it—loading the gel packs, salt tablets, Nuun tablets, and spare tubes—I wanted to get in that practice swim.

"Honey, what do you want to do now?" I asked.

"The kids are hungry. I think we should take them to lunch."

"Do you mind if I get in a quick swim before we go? I want to swim the course and make sure the wetsuit is in good shape and doesn't have any leaks."

"How long is a quick swim?"

"Only about thirty to forty-five minutes."

Death stare. "Do you see these three kids here? They are starving and want some lunch. You are not doing a forty-five-minute practice swim. You are going to McDonald's."

"Honey, I can't eat McDonald's the day before the—"

Death stare.

"Yes, dear. McDonald's will be fine."

TIP: You'll have a number of tasks to get done in the days before the race—register, drop off your bike, prep your bike, take a practice swim in your wetsuit to test the suit and get a feel for the conditions—and you don't want to drag your family through that. You'll be waiting in lines to register, and it takes time. If you've billed the weekend as a family vacation, this will not go over well. Either give them a real vacation or bring someone that your spouse will enjoy spending time with—a best friend, mother, or a Swede named Sven. Let them enjoy the festivities, fine dining, kid activities, and such with a companion and not make them follow you around multiple lines waiting for you to free up so you can focus on them. You'll want to focus on the race, not worry about making sure your family is taken care of.

That night, as I ate about two thousand calories of beef, fish, and pasta at the hotel restaurant's special race buffet, Karoline reminded me that she had an awards dinner for work the following evening. "Remember, I have to be at the dinner at

6 p.m. We have to leave right away. My team is getting an award, and I can't miss this dinner."

She was putting a lot of faith in me to finish the race within the six hours I said I would. "Don't worry, sweetie. I'll be done a little after five hours. That should be around 1 p.m. Plenty of time to get you home so you can shower and change and get to the dinner."

I knew this was a stretch. She knew it too. We were going to be cutting it close. If something happened during the race, and I took longer than I predicted, which was probable since I always predicted I'd do better than I ever did, she'd never make her dinner. And I'd be a dead man walking.

After dinner, we went back to the hotel room, and I began laying out my clothes and equipment for the morning. Karoline pulled out a little plastic shopping bag. "I got you something," she said, eyes gleaming mischievously. "It's the fortieth anniversary of Ironman, and they were selling these commemorative shirts. I thought you'd like one."

She handed me the bag. I pulled out a beautiful, sleek, black bike racing jersey. It had the fortieth anniversary logo on it. I had seen it throughout the day and had commented on how much I liked it. But I couldn't justify spending money on it, so I just admired it from afar. "Consider it a late birthday present," she said. "You're going to do great tomorrow. I'm so proud of you."

I don't deserve you, I thought. I packed it in my backpack of clothes for the morning. I would wear that shirt in the race. This was one last-minute race decision that I was thrilled to make. The shirt could chafe me until my nipples were bloody hamburger bits, but I would make sure that shirt was on me when I crossed the finish line.

I woke at 3:30 a.m. the next morning, baby bird still pecking, and fumbled around the hotel room in the dark, careful not to wake the sleeping cherubs. Though I had packed everything the night before and put it in a designated spot near the door, I worried that I'd forget something.

Most everything I'd need that day was already on site in plastic bags hung in the transition area—bike shoes, helmet, running shoes, shorts, shirt, and so on. What wasn't there already—my wetsuit, snacks, extra water, and bike pump—I now carried in another plastic bag.

I trudged down to the hotel's café and store, which had opened early to serve breakfast to athletes. I nodded groggily at my fellow racers in their Under Armour and flip-flops, holding bike pumps. I ordered a bacon, egg, and cheese sandwich, a banana, and a coffee. Then I hopped on the shuttle that would take me to the swim start. I had to walk about a mile through a residential neighborhood to Great Marsh Park, which served as the bike holding area and swim start location.

I looked out at the bay. The sky was pewter and ominous, and the water tea-colored and rough. I shivered at the thought of having to jump in it and swim in an hour. The weather reports called for rain at some point in the day. Yuck.

Karoline and the kids would take a later shuttle and watch the race from the marshy, muddy park. I said a silent prayer for the rain to hold off until after the race—not so much for me, but because I knew if Karoline was stuck in the rain for five hours, it would not be a pleasant ride home. And if the weather slowed me down and made us late for her dinner, it would be like riding through the River Styx to my death.

Thankfully, the rain held off. Aside from having some stomach issues during the run and having a sore throat the entire way, I finished in 5:43—a respectable showing that still left plenty of time to get Karoline home.

TIP: If you're anxious about doing your first Ironman or Half Ironman and want to find an "easier" one, or you want the best chance at a PR, pick Maryland/Eagleman. The course is as flat as a twelve-year-old boy's chest and as fast as a sixteen-year-old boy in heat. Still grueling, still a grind, but less so than other Ironman races.

I met Karoline and the kids at the finish line, and then we all went to pick up my bike in the holding pen so we could get back to the hotel, load the car, and leave. But the pen wasn't open yet. There was a line waiting to get in that stretched a quarter of a mile. "What's going on?" I asked the couple in front of me.

"They're only allowing a few people in at a time for some reason."

"What do you mean?" I asked. "This will take forever."

I felt Karoline's eyes burning a hole in the back of my head. I turned to tell her how sorry I was. "You need to do something," she said. I wanted to beg the Ironman volunteers to let me cut the line and get my bike. That would have really endeared me to the one hundred people in front of me who were anxious to get their bikes too.

We waited, hoping they would speed it up. Karoline stewed. I thought that I might have been better off if I had drowned in the swim.

Forty-five minutes later, I finally got in the holding area and retrieved my bike. We packed the car in a panic…and then sat in Sunday afternoon traffic on the one main road leaving the Eastern Shore and leading to the Chesapeake Bay Bridge. The Southwest ad echoed in my head. *Wanna get away?* Yes, please.

Ten minutes after we got in the car, the skies opened, and a torrential rain pounded the windshield. Thank God it had held off, and the family hadn't gotten caught in a monsoon while they waited for me. One small win.

Karoline made her dinner—only thirty minutes late—and I learned a valuable lesson. Ironmans are hard enough. Don't make them any harder by being a dumbass and giving your family a terrible, horrible, no good, very bad day.

CHAPTER 6
THE VALUE OF TOILET PAPER

Life is on the wire,
and everything else is just waiting.
— Karl Wallenda

Miles 6–10 (8.4–12.4)

My stomach began gurgling around mile six. The dam was about to burst. Would I be able to make it to the next porta potty? There wasn't a great place to pull off to the side of the road and go. I'd have to endure and squeeze and just find a way to make it to a better spot.

I felt the trickle roll down my leg. *I'm going to smell beautiful after this race.* Finally, two hundred yards ahead on my right, in a carved-out scenic overlook—the Mount Van Hoevenberg Recreation Area—I spied a porta potty. I pedaled as if I was in a sprint to the finish line with my fiercest rival and that my life itself was riding on the outcome.

I threw my bike down next to the dull, grey, rectangular box that, at this moment, I valued more than all of my possessions. I would have traded the deed to my house and given my first-born son for that simple gray box that smelled like a rotting whale corpse that had baked in the sun on the beach for three weeks.

Please, God, let there be nobody in there. The handle of the door indicated "green," meaning it was vacant. *Thank you, Lord.* I ripped off my shirt. (My bike bib had suspenders, and I could not get my pants off without first taking off my shirt—I'd have to reconsider that next time I know I'm going to need to take a dozen craps during a race.)

I pulled my pants down, crouched, and imitated a plane dumping extra fuel to lighten its load and complete its trip. Relieved, I reached for toilet paper to clean up the undercarriage. There was no toilet paper. "How is there no toilet paper this early in the race?!" I wailed.

Riding a bike 112 miles after swimming for two and a half is not comfortable. Every muscle in your body aches. Your neck feels like it just went through an MMA fight. Your quads are in open revolt. Your wrists wish they had carpal tunnel instead of what they're going through during the ride. Your bottom is raw. The last thing you need is wet, sticky stink following you around for the next hundred miles.

I put my shirt on and pulled my pants up only three quarters of the way, hopeful that I could find some leaves or blades of grass to sop up the shit on my backside. I spied an SUV parked in the overlook. A man and a woman exited the vehicle. The man popped open the back door and pulled out a stroller. The woman reached into a side door and pulled out...A BABY!

I clip-clopped over to them in my bike shoes. "Hi," I started. "Um, this is embarrassing, but the porta potty ran out of toilet paper. Would you happen to have some baby wipes you could spare?"

What if they said no? Would I beg? Would I offer to trade them a strawberry-banana power gel? Would I threaten to squirt the baby with my water bottle?

I was grateful that it didn't come to this. They were more than happy to give me a handful of baby wipes. God is good. I returned to the porta potty that I had just destroyed (olfactorily speaking) and spent the next ten minutes cleaning myself off. I emerged from the toxic test tube, breathed in the fresh air, sipped my Spark sports drink, reset my chi, and returned to the race.

It started to rain.

Perfect. I was about to begin one of the most treacherous descents in the entire canon of Ironman races, and now a wet, slick road would make it even more harrowing.

CHAPTER 7

GO FAST, TAKE CHANCES

Are you in earnest? Seize this very minute.
Boldness has genius, power, and magic in it.
Only engage, and then the mind grows heated—
begin it, and then the work will be completed.

—Johann von Goethe

Miles 10–14 (12.4–16.4)

I lived for five years in Santa Clarita, California, a valley surrounded on all sides by the Sierra Pelona, San Gabriel, and Santa Susana Mountains. To paraphrase Senator Lloyd Bentsen, I trained in those mountains. I knew those mountains. They were good mountains. You, Sir Adirondacks, are not those mountains.

I used to climb for miles up the Sierras, deep into the Angeles National Forest. Up the winding roads, just me and the desert and the mountain peaks in one hundred-degree heat. Grueling. Death. Then after two or three hours of non-stop climbing, I'd turn around and go down. Then it was *exhilarating*.

I'd bomb down the mountain, reaching speeds of nearly 50 mph as I twisted around the rocky walls. No timid rider, I.

The four-mile descent down Route 73 to the town of Keene during the Ironman, however, scares me to death.

One reason is you share the road with dozens of other riders. You not only have to worry about you and your bike, but everyone else's bike too. I once saw a rider's water bottle fall onto the road into the path of an unfortunate soul whose wheel caught it.

The wheel wobbled, the bike teetered, and then the man hit the pavement, bouncing twenty yards down the road in a perfect reenactment of Evel Knievel's Caesars Palace Fountain jump until he slammed into the stone wall on the side of the road.

You also placed your life and limbs in the components of your bike. A brake cable could snap—and I'd had that happen before—and the only way to effectively stop on that hill would be to introduce your bike to a tree. A tire could puncture—a common occurrence—and cause your bike to skid and fishtail and throw you off like a bucking bull.

This hill could not just wreck your day. It could wreck your ability to walk without a limp for your remaining years. Despite this, some riders showed no fear and pedaled furiously down, maxing out at speeds around 60 mph.

Believe me, you don't need to go that fast to do serious damage. My worst accident occurred when I was commuting to work at Disney, in Burbank, California. I was clipping into my pedals and wasn't watching the road. The last thing I remember is seeing my front wheel roll into a sewage drain.

I woke up in an ambulance looking like I'd tried to kiss an oncoming train. I had been riding about 5 mph.

"They're crazy," Uncle Bob said of the downhill speedsters. "They hit one pebble, and they're done. Done. It's not worth it."

But wait, there's more! To up the death or serious bodily injury ante, not only do you share the road with other riders, but you also share the road with *oncoming cars and trucks.*

Yes, you read that right. One lane of the road is open to vehicular traffic. While you're screaming down the hill hoping not to hit a rock or slick spot, cars buzz past you going up the hill. A line of orange traffic cones delineating where cars and bikes never shall cross is all that's keeping you from a mosquito-splat-on-the-windshield experience. I'm not a physicist, but I do believe the car would win that encounter.

The real threat, however—the silent assassins that are most likely to wreck your day—are all the road ornaments. By this, I mean all the debris that is either already on, or ends up on, the road.

I told you about the water bottle. Riders also contend with the possibility of rocks, broken glass, potholes, and sticks, as well as slick gel packs, tangled bike tubes, Clif Bar wrappers, and other detritus that are the result of reaching high speeds on a bumpy pavement.

We've all been behind a pickup or dump truck on its way to the dump that hasn't tied down its cargo very well or forgoes a tarp. It rumbles along, leaving a trail of wood chips, scrap metal, paper cups, or packing peanuts in its wake.

That's your potential experience on the Keene descent—except instead of wood chips that fall harmlessly underneath your car's tire or packing peanuts that swirl innocently in the wind, it's little metal CO_2 cartridges bouncing off the road into your gears or under your one-inch bike tire, sending you on a journey to the guardrail and a first-class ride in an ambulance.

Route 73 was repaved in 2016, mitigating the peril caused by the friendly little ride-killers falling from bouncing bikes roaring along at 40 and 50 mph. So the hill technically shouldn't have been as white-knuckle as my previous races.

But the 2018 Ironman Lake Placid expedition down that hill was the most terrifying ride I'd experience in my life.

I crested the hill and began the four-mile descent, and I thought of those ski jumpers. We had watched a practice while at the jumps during the week. They practiced by jumping into a giant pool, working out their mistakes while crashing into the soft bubbling water.

There was no such practice for biking down a hill. No pool or pile of mattresses. My bike began to pick up speed, and I gave my brakes a little squeeze to test them. At this point, they were an ornament adorning my bike, with as much utility as streamers on the handlebars of a five-year-old girl's Huffy.

A few riders whizzed by me. Idiots. What was the point? They were risking serious injury to save a minute or two in a fourteen-hour day.

I recalled my friend Dwayne's fun adventure during a race in Aspen. He didn't make a turn and woke up in a ditch in the woods. How long had he been there? He didn't know. But he got back on his bike and finished the race. No concussion was going to stop him from getting a finisher's medal and tee shirt!

My glasses kept fogging up, and I couldn't see the road. This didn't bother me so much when I was going uphill. But going down a steep descent is when you want to be able to see every divot, pothole, rock, or leaf on the road. Why didn't I take them off, you ask? Have you ever watched the Kentucky Derby? Riders wear goggles, and at the end of the race, you know why. They are covered in dirt and mud.

It's not quite that bad, but debris—bugs, dirt, twigs, and any assortment of items—often fly into your eyes. Glasses aren't just for the glare; they also protect your eyes from flying debris.

I rode blind for a hundred feet or so, but it reminded me of the time that Jim and I climbed on a roof of a cottage in Cape Cod, drank a bottle of Jameson, and then decided we wanted to see *Waterworld*.

We bribed a friend to drive us to the theater by paying for his ticket and popcorn. Ten minutes into the film, Jim and I looked at each other. "I can't see the screen. Can you?" I asked.

"I wasn't going to say anything...but, no...I can't see a thing," Jim answered. "Let's go." We were so hammered that we couldn't see the screen, so we ditched the theater and directed the disappointed friend to take us to Salty's Seafood Diner, where we tore into a plate of chicken wings, fried calamari, and mozzarella sticks.

I was at the same level of visual impairment going down a mountain road at 40 mph as I was watching *Waterworld* that night. Like *Waterworld* (the film and my viewing of it), the whole operation should have been aborted, and I should have found a Salty's in the Adirondacks to sober up.

I took off the glasses. Better. If a rock flew into my eye, so be it. Suddenly, a wicked crosswind blew my bike ten feet across the road. Thank God another rider hadn't been coming along next to me, or I would have taken him out like Maximum Security took out War of Will in the Kentucky Derby. It took all my strength to keep the bike from careening off the road down the embankment into Cascade Lake.

I picked the wrong race to try new wheels that catch wind like a fucking sail. Wind gusts continued to hammer me as I picked up more speed, and my bike jerked around like a kite. The sensation was not unlike experiencing severe turbulence on a plane:

The pilot asks that you fasten your seatbelts. We're going to hit a small pocket of turbulence.

Then the plane drops suddenly like you're on the Tower of Terror at Disney World. My bike was being pushed all over the road—a horizontal hallway of terror. Had I been driving a car, I would have been pulled over for reckless driving.

TIP: Don't ride aero wheels in a hurricane, especially if you only weigh 130 pounds.

The wind worried me. CO_2 cartridges flying into my face worried me. But the wet roads nearly paralyzed me.

Biking on wet roads is like running on ice: a bad idea. I biked once with a cycling club in Washington, DC, that met a couple mornings a week before work. We used to bike through Rock Creek Park, a winding, hilly route.

One morning, I tried to navigate a turn down a hill and hit a patch of wet leaves. The wheels skidded right out from under me, and I ended up in a ditch underneath my mangled bike.

Another time, I got caught in a rainstorm. Sopping wet and cold, I should have stopped and ditched the bike for an Uber. Instead, I pressed on and didn't see a turn on a downhill and ended up going up an embankment into a thicket of bushes and got a nasty gash across my arm. Once, I hydroplaned through a puddle, lost control of the bike, and crashed on the pavement, leaving me with a nasty road rash. The hard road shredded my skin like a cheese grater.

I didn't have a good history with rain and wet roads. Wet roads are slick roads. Wet roads make your brakes nice decorations. Wet roads lead to body casts.

I was prepared to use my five-year-old son's method of stopping when riding his balance bike. He would just put the toes of his sneakers against the pavement as if he had stoppers on them like old-time roller skates. While his sneaker bill was quite large from having to replace ground-up shoes every couple of weeks, I have to admit it was an effective braking method.

I decided employing this method in an Ironman would have been totally embarrassing and probably not as effective in this situation. I chose instead to make my body a sail to catch as much headwind as possible to slow me down at least a little.

I stood on the bike, puffed my chest out, and made myself as big as possible—not in a peacock displaying dominance way…more like a meek downhill skier who goes down a black diamond hill by mistake, and then, terrified, continues down in that snowplow position with the ski tips pointed inward to go as slow as possible. Other racers could tuck down to get as aerodynamic and go as fast as they pleased. I was seeking to survive and advance to the long flat section of the bike course that gave some respite before the real climbing began.

The gusts of crosswinds continued to whip me around the road, but there was also steady wind at my face the entire descent. I rode the rest of the way downhill spread out like Eddie the Eagle off a ski jump, and though I may have looked silly, I made it to the bottom safe and sound. No crash. I had come out of the Keene descent unscathed and would not be denied the bliss of the pain and suffering ahead.

CHAPTER 8
CRASH AND BURN

The race is won by the rider who can suffer the most.
— Eddy Merckx

Miles 15–24 (17.4–26.4) – Keene to Jay
The Flats. Finally.

Route 73 rambles along toward the town of Keene. The view is forest and fields and farmhouses. Once you start seeing more homes clustered close together, you know you're near the town.

I passed the Cedar Run Bakery and Market and thought back to those days before I got into Ironman when I'd bike simply for the joy of it. How nice it was to pedal without a care for time or speed—when I'd move at a leisurely clip, take in the scenery, and stop at an inviting bakery or coffee shop like Cedar Run to get a scone or iced coffee before bounding off again to wherever my mood took me.

I crossed over a small bridge over the craggy Ausable River and then turned left onto Route 9N, heading to the town of Jay, which I learned was named after John Jay, the governor of

New York when it was formed. Its town motto: home of the covered bridge.

Aside from the famous covered bridge and wilderness, there wasn't much to Jay, which had a population of 2,506. Once upon a time, however, a magical land was contained within its borders. Once upon a time, this unassuming little village could lay claim to one of America's very first theme parks. A full year before Walt Disney opened Disneyland, another former animator and Hollywood filmmaker by the name of Arto Monaco opened a new amusement park in the tiny hamlet of Upper Jay.

Like Walt, for whom he had once worked, Arto was a creative visionary who wanted to build a place for kids and families. That place became the Land of Makebelieve, where children were encouraged to use their imaginations. Think low-key and whimsical—more Mr. Rogers low-budget Neighborhood of Makebelieve than the grandeur of Disney.

Still, the Land of Makebelieve had a castle, a riverboat, pirate ships, steam trains, several fairytale houses, a stagecoach, and an old western town. At least it had all these things until a devastating winter flood from the adjacent Ausable River dealt the park a death blow, and it closed for good in 1979. For all his vision, old Arto didn't foresee the danger of placing his magic land in a flood plain.

Pre-Ironman days, my own whimsical curiosity would have taken me on an adventure to find the remnants of this land. I would have biked until I came across the tattered entrance and located the grounds and shells of the saloon and saddlery of the old western town—now an overgrown ghost town.

In a race, you don't take adventures. You hardly notice the scenery. You're not admiring the landscape or stopping to explore the points of interest. You're just focused on the road, the young guy who just blew by you...and the pain. As I biked up Route 9N, I hardly noticed the Ausable River snaking alongside the road to my left, nary a foot deep—more rocky stream than raging river that might wash away an entire amusement park.

Channeling Arto, I tried to use my imagination to make believe I was sitting in a steakhouse, eating a filet and drinking a cold beer served by Kate Upton while simultaneously getting a deep tissue massage and a coconut scrub facial from Margot Robbie.

TIP: Find coping mechanisms to get through the tough times. Jim sings to himself to ease his anxiety during the swim. Some focus on loved ones or friends who have battled or continue to battle diseases or illness and use their struggles as inspiration. Some think about making their kids proud. Others visualize themselves crossing the finish line. I imagine Margot Robbie rubbing my temples and Kate Upton handing me a Blue Moon.

At the "town center" for Jay, I turned onto Route 86 toward Wilmington.

Miles 25–29 (27.4–31.4) - Jay to Wilmington
This section features arguably the most difficult climb on the whole bike course. I clicked into my lowest gear and settled in for more than a mile of the steep uphill—the meat grinder that spits out athletes like my daughter spits out medicine. It is here that I see many riders get off their bikes and walk. They almost walk as fast as those still on the saddle, creeping ever-so-slowly up, up, up.

It is here where the legs first start to burn. Really burn. As Jim always says about upcoming races, the only thing you can guarantee in an Ironman is…pain.

Angelo Fausto Coppi, the Italian cycling legend who many consider the greatest ever, said, simply, "Cycling is suffering."

Eddy Merckx, who racked up an untouchable record of wins during his decorated career, put it this way: "Cyclists live with pain. If you can't handle it, you will win nothing. The race is won by the rider who can suffer the most."

I was in no danger of winning. I did not like to suffer. At least not enough. I allowed for some suffering, but I wasn't ready to take it to the lengths Coppi or Merckx had. Or Tom Simpson.

Simpson was a twenty-nine-year-old cycling pro from the UK who was at the peak of his powers during the 1967 Tour de France. Britain's first celebrity cyclist was climbing the fabled Mont Ventoux in the Alps during the thirteenth stage of the Tour when he collapsed from exhaustion and died. He literally rode himself to death.

The climb on Route 86 toward Wilmington was certainly not the Beast of Provence. But it was a bitch. It could suck the life out of you in a hurry. I was not ready to die for the race, but I was also unwilling to cede to the hill by getting off and walking. I still had enough juice to stay on the bike.

I made it to the top of the hill and collapsed into my aero bars, coasting on the downhill, giving myself a brief respite. I made it to the out-and-back on Haselton Road. This was a narrow stretch that was fairly flat and shaded by towering evergreens. It should have been uneventful. Then my stomach started gurgling again.

I rode along the winding road and prayed for an aide station to appear soon. After about four miles, I spied a porta potty in a sandy cut-out along the road. One lonely bathroom standing sentry among the pines. There was a line. Balls. I did a quick calculus about whether I should try to make it to the next porta potty or turn off and wait in line.

As I started to pass the sandy lot, I determined that my bladder would not deign to wait until the next porta potty, so I jerked the bike left. If you've ever ridden a bike in deep, wet sand, you know that this did not end well.

My front wheel hit the sand and wobbled and skidded. My sweet Cervelo that I had cleaned the night before with a toothbrush, some soapy water, and a rag, careened over and threw me into the sand. Sand in my mouth. Sand in my eyes. Sand in my helmet. As much as I don't enjoy chewing sand, this did not bother me so much. Sand in my teeth was not a problem.

Sand in my bike was a problem. My Cervelo and all of the contents that hitherto had been on it were sprawled and scattered across the sandy lot. One tip I had learned through the years was to open all nutrition so it would be easier to eat during a race. So, I'd rip off part of the wrapper on my Stingers, blocks, and gels to be able to access them without fuss. The peanut butter, jelly, chia seed, and cinnamon sandwich poked out of the unsealed Ziploc bag so I didn't have to waste precious energy trying to dig it out while careening down the road at over 20 mph.

Brilliant strategy if you don't crash. But now all that food—as well as the Nuun electrolyte tablets—was covered in sand. Grainy and gritty. Quite inedible.

As for my bike, every gear, sprocket, chain link, brake pad, nook, and cranny was infiltrated by sand. The super-duper water bottle holder that I had bought and had installed behind my seat for the outrageous price of $74 had smashed on the ground and broken apart.

I kneeled in the sand for a moment and viewed the carcass of my bike and the scattered ashes of my food. Was this where my race would end? You dumb bastard, I thought. You know what happens when you bike in deep sand.

My stomach reminded me of a more acute need.

I left the bike as is and waited in line for the porta potty. Once I got in, I stripped off my shirt. Bloody hell. There was nowhere to hang it. I threw it over my shoulders. I crouched for a few moments, savoring the sweet relief. Then a loud knock on the door. A woman's voice. "Are you almost done in there?"

Do you think I like spending time in this 120-degree box that smells like Andre the Giant's onesie after WrestleMania?

When I finished, I looked at the explosion I had left on the seat. Gross. I pulled some toilet paper to wipe it down. Loud knocking. "Hurry up in there. Some of us would like to get back to the race today." The same woman.

Fine. I left the porta potty without cleaning the seat. "It's all yours. Enjoy," I said to her as I exited.

She hadn't even closed the door when she poked her head out and shouted. "You're a disgusting pig!"

I stuck my tongue out at the unsympathetic, impatient wench. So mature. But Ironman does things to you.

Then, like a dad looking for a lost Lego underneath the kitchen table, I got on my hands and knees and started searching for the microscopic screws. Even if I found them, my Allen wrench set had broken apart, making it questionable if I'd be able to screw them back on.

A couple people came over and asked if I was okay or needed help. I was fine, physically, but I wasn't sure my bike was.

Sidebar: Athletes in an Ironman are a generous and kind sort who are quick to offer help or lend you equipment. This is almost always the case except in one specific circumstance: the swim. During the swim, athletes have no problem drowning you if you are in their way. But then, if you're lying in the sand fumbling with your bike, that same guy that swam over you will stop to see if you need a hand.

I waved them off. I had found the screws, and the remnants of my Allen wrench would work well enough to screw the bottle holder back on.

I looked over my bike. Aside from the fact that it looked like it had been buried in the desert for ten years, there seemed to be no structural issues. No flat. No chain snafus. I tried to clip into the pedals. I couldn't. The bottoms of my shoes were full of sand. I used the rest of my water to wash them out.

Miles 30–45 (32.4–47.4)

I clipped in and, with a wobbly push, got back on the course. My brakes were all gunked up. Not working well. At least I was on the flats. Haselton is an out and back, and I prayed that there was an aide station at the turnaround, because I hadn't seen one on the section of Haselton I had already ridden, so I knew if there wasn't one somewhere within the two miles up ahead, it was going to be awhile. I needed to wash out my bike parts, and I was out of water.

Have you ever gone to the beach, gotten sand on your sandwich, and taken a big bite? You get that awful unexpected crunch, like chewing broken glass. You then spit it out and wash your mouth out with a beverage. Well, my bike had swallowed a bucketful of sand and was now gagging on it as I trudged around the Haselton turnaround and headed back to Route 86. It needed a large beverage, and I didn't have one for it.

I passed the sandy scene of the crime and gave it the finger. Then I realized that I had focused so much on my gagging gears that I hadn't noticed that—for the first time since that morning—my stomach felt normal. The ten minutes that I spent in that box that smelled like Ndamukong Suh's jock strap after a three-hour NFL game might have finally cleared all the chaos out of my tummy.

I eventually made it to an aide station. Aide stations consist of tables full of gel packs, bananas, pretzels, Clif Bars, PowerBars, blocks, goos, and grapes. Volunteers stand along the side of the road and offer you water, Gatorade, Coca-Cola, cups of ice, and sometimes chicken broth.

I nearly took out a line of volunteers as I came in hot and couldn't unclip from my pedals due to the sand. Water cups went flying as they caught me and slowed me to a stop. I apologized and told them my issue. One volunteer, a middle-aged moustache-wearing man named Steve, walked me over to the side and started pouring water from water bottles over my bike gears and chain and brakes.

TIP: Thank volunteers every chance you get. They give you water, direction, sunscreen, and encouragement. They help you take off your clothes and put on your clothes. They touch things no human should have to touch. They keep you safe. Without them, you'd never get past the starting gate.

With good cheer, Steve cleaned the remaining sand from my shoes and filled up my empty water bottles. I restocked my bento box with a few gels and blocks, cautiously ate half a banana, and went on my way.

CHAPTER 9
THE WILDERNESS

I went to the woods because I wished to live deliber-
ately, to front only the essential facts of life. And see
if I could not learn what it had to teach and not,
when I came to die, discover that I had not lived.

— Henry David Thoreau

Miles 43–44 (45.4–46.4)

I turned onto Route 86 in Wilmington, the final thirteen
miles of the first loop. This section featured the beastly Three
Bears, a dreaded series of hills. It was the part of the race where
if you felt good for the first forty-three miles, you would soon
be disabused of that feeling. Well, I'd felt like shit for the first
forty-three miles, so things weren't looking good for me.

I slumped over my aero bars, dreading what was ahead.
Sheets of rain continued pummeling me—drip, drip, drip—
against my bare arms and legs, like a primitive form of water-
boarding. My feet were drenched and cold and sore—a soreness like a continuous muscle cramp that you can't shake out.
My sunglasses were useless; though they weren't necessary to
diminish the brightness of the sun, they could have been use-

ful to keep the raindrops from stinging my eyes had they not remained fogged up.

TIP: Invest in good sunglasses—particularly ones with photo chromatic lenses that automatically adjust tint levels for light conditions. After racing for many years with Ray-Ban Wayfarers, I finally smartened up and got sunglasses made for cycling. I went with the Ultra Remount from Performance Bicycle. These have lenses that lighten and darken up to 38 percent based on light transmission. They also have anti-fog treatment on the inside to keep the lens clear and adjustable nose pads that provide a no-slip grip. During a long ride, there will be times when the sun is shining bright on your face and times when tree cover will create shadows on the road. You want to be able to see well in the shadows and not worry about switching out lenses.

I passed the restaurant at which Jim and I had eaten breakfast al fresco the morning before, which was aptly named Up A Creek. And seventy-five feet beyond Up A Creek, I came upon the Wilderness Inn, warmly glowing and sitting snugly among the pines. It happened to be where I was lodging. I stopped in front of it, and contemplated pulling in, stripping off my wet clothes, putting on a fire, and burrowing under the blankets of my bed.

I discovered the Wilderness Inn in 2011 when Jim and I volunteered and camped at the North Pole, which was down the street from it. It's a rustic set of cabins in Wilmington, New York, ten miles outside of Lake Placid village. For the Ironman in 2012—to save money but not have the threat of a tent collapsing on me—I booked it for my accommodations.

The inn's catchphrase is "Roughing it in Style," and its cabins have pastoral names like Balsam, Norway, Cedar, Hemlock, and Aspen. If you like knotty pine walls, old stone fireplaces, "a serene, wooded alpine setting" and a "quaint, cozy atmosphere," the Wilderness Inn is for you.

Some of the cabins have full kitchens—a big selling point if you want to cook very specific Ironman meals to meet precise nutritional needs. If you prefer that someone else do the cooking, the inn also has an on-site restaurant that allows you to order a prime rib and baked potato combo, drink a wild concoction dreamed up and named Blue Iris by June, the saucy and sarcastic bartender who has been there since 1975, and stumble a mere twenty yards over a few tree roots to your bed.

All this is packaged in an atmosphere of knotty-pine wonder, with walls that are adorned with year-round Christmas lights and 1930s ski equipment. It is an Adirondack ambience wet dream.

An interesting fact I learned about the Wilderness Inn from a server one night and confirmed by June is that the Soviet press stayed there during the 1980 Winter Olympics. After the KGB vetted the place, the members of the press crammed into the cabins for two weeks—twelve men alone stuffed themselves into the snug Balsam, a one-room deal with two double beds. They spent the time drinking enough Stoli vodka from the restaurant to fuel a jetliner, bragging about how dominant the Soviet men's hockey team was.

The night the U.S. men's hockey team won the Miracle on Ice against the Soviet machine, the Russians graciously bought every round. The owner of the inn told them they could drink only American drinks. The Soviet press abided by this rule and got obliterated on Jack Daniels. They could drink vodka as if they had a wooden leg, downing glass after glass and looking as sober as a cyclist during the Keene descent. But they did not handle their whiskey nearly as well.

The Balsam was the cabin I was currently sharing with Sherpa Jim, and where I was now contemplating abandoning the race to hole up and drink my pain away like the Russians.

In 2012, I stayed in the Spruce. I had wanted some extra space so my mom, my aunt Norma, and my niece Molly could join Karoline and me, and the Spruce cabin has three bedrooms—each with a single and a double bed—a full kitchen, an eight-seat dining table, and a fireplace. All for only $175 a night. For me, pre-kids, this was ideal.

For my friend Jim, with two young charges at the time, being right in the heart of the village near the expo and all the activities was paramount. So he paid $230 a night with a five-night minimum for a room at the Best Western Adirondack

Inn. His mom and dad booked a separate room at Crowne Plaza at the top of a steep hill overlooking the town for a similar price.

My Uncle Bob always made fun of me for staying at the Wilderness Inn. He had rented a gorgeous home a half mile outside Lake Placid village for $7,000 a night. His house was tastefully infused with a more upscale Adirondack vibe than the Wilderness—less rustic, more spa.

It was big enough that it could have housed the entire Soviet hockey team plus the press. It had also been host to famous guests. Bruce Springsteen had stayed there a few weeks prior. As it was, Bob's kids and grandkids came up and ably filled the house.

Unlike Uncle Bob, I couldn't afford to rent a multimillion-dollar home and couldn't justify spending what it cost to rent anything near town.

At the Wilderness Inn, however, I could get a cabin with two double beds and a fireplace for $75 a night, which is what Jim and I paid for the Balsam. I have enough guilt spending thousands of dollars on bikes and flights and registration that anything I can do to lessen that guilt is a good decision. The Wilderness is a cozy, comfy homage to guilt reduction.

TIP: If concerned about mounting costs, find a Wilderness Inn—a cheap place a little farther out of town. Or look for a local campground and pitch a tent. You'll have a great time and save a ton of

money. If you have kids, they will love camping out. Campgrounds are built for kids and have tons of amenities and activities for them. If you're concerned about comfort and convenience, spend a little more money and rent a house in the town within walking distance to the Ironman Village and the race start and finish. Your spouse and family can walk back and forth to the house from all the activities, restaurants, and shops. This will make for a much better experience for them as parking is difficult and roads are blocked during race day.

For Bob, with kids and toddler grandkids watching the race, schlepping back and forth for naptime and lunchtime and other assorted times, a house in town was necessary. "You've got to involve the whole family," he says. "The guys who have trouble at home or have to stop doing Ironman don't incorporate their families."

Uncle Bob incorporates his family better than anyone I know, especially at Lake Placid. He always rents a nice house right in the village, or at the edge of it. He and my Aunt Connie and a group of Ironman friends they've met through years go out to eat each night and enjoy the shops and sites of Lake Placid, and his three daughters make a vacation out of it and bring their kids.

I heeded Bob's advice about involving family, and for the 2016 race, I was prepared to rent a bunch of cabins at the Wilderness Inn for any family member who wanted to join. My mother, Aunt Norma, and Molly were planning to come again. My brother Chris, sister-in-law Kathleen, and their daughter Brianna were also joining that year, as were Karoline's parents, her brother Andy, and sister and brother-in-law, Kerney and Sam.

I told my Aunt Connie my plan to rent out all the cabins at Wilderness and give everyone a great time, so proud of myself for incorporating family into Ironman, just like Uncle Bob recommended. "You're crazy," she said.

"What are you talking about?" I asked. She pointed out that this time, unlike 2012, Karoline would be hauling two kids with her—a three-year-old and one-year-old. Then she told me that thirteen or fourteen hours watching a race was almost as exhausting as the race itself, and that it would be nice to give my seventy-one-year-old mom a place in town to retreat to and rest.

"We're not renting the house we rented this year (they were upgrading to the Bruce Springsteen house). It's available for 2016. Do you want me to call the realtor and hold it for you?"

"How much is it?"

"$5,100. But it's worth it. With Karoline and the kids, you want to be in town, not out in the woods ten miles away."

I gulped hard. I could buy a car for that. Or even better, a new bike. "You really think so? That's a lot of money. I'd spend less than $1,000 renting out the entire Wilderness compound."

"Yeah, but you're ten miles out on a street that is blocked to road traffic during the race. What if Karoline needs to take Fintan back for a nap, or wants to just sit and rest for a while? Where's she gonna go? Let me give you some advice. Spend the money."

So I listened to my aunt. I walked down to Merrill L. Thomas Real Estate, a little cottage on Main Street whose offices overlooked the lake, with my checkbook in hand.

"Am I doing the right thing?" I asked the kindly, energetic sales lady as I pulled out a check to pay the deposit.

"Oh, your family will be thrilled," she said, smiling broadly. "They'll be right in the heart of the action, and you have plenty of space." I handed her the check, hesitantly. "Your Aunt Connie is a wise woman. I think your wife will be much happier in this location than ten miles out in Wilmington."

"Will she be tickled when I tell her our kids can't go to college because I've spent their tuition on this house?"

She laughed. "You'll see," she said in the same way I spoke to Peter when I tried to convince him he'd be happy we took him to the National Art Gallery. "You'll be glad you did it," she assured me in a squinty-eyed whisper.

The house was a 2,400-square foot, four-bedroom, 3.5 bath house with a fully furnished deck, a grill, and a small, private backyard. The location—on Elm Street, two hundred yards up a hill from Main Street in Lake Placid and a quarter of a mile from where my aunt set up camp on Mirror Lake Drive—was perfect.

My aunt was right: renting that house for that 2016 race when I had extended family was worth every penny.

But for this current race, where I was joined only by my Ironman enablers Jim, Mark, and Jeff, who were graciously serving as Sherpas and could "rough it in style," the Wilderness Inn was the better choice.

Now I sat on the grass in front of the Wilderness, a few yards from the road where other racers slogged through the wind and rain, squeezed a gel—banana flavor—into my gullet, and took a few sips of my electrolyte drink, contemplating my next move. The Wilderness beckoned. God, how nice a hot shower would feel at this moment. Some people, like Uncle Bob's running partner Renee, can just pack it up, quit the race, get a shower and a nice meal, and join all the supporters cheering the racers. They don't mind a DNF one bit.

DNF. Did Not Finish. Those are the scarlet letters attached to your name if you quit the race or don't make the cut-off times. Most people are devastated to get a DNF. Some are relieved and happy to have it over with. I wouldn't be suicidal if I didn't finish, but I'd sure be disappointed with myself.

So why did I gravitate toward the suffering option? It would have been so easy to end the pain and go into the warm cabin, shower, and then head to the bar and have Jane pour me something to make me forget my name.

The answer? I wanted to hear Mike Reilly announce that Russell Newell was an Ironman. I wanted that stupid five-dollar medal. It meant something to get that hung over your neck. It meant enough that—beyond my powers to stop them—tears streamed down my cheeks every time it happened.

I hopped back on the bike and pressed on, girded by the cheering fans in front of the Wilderness Inn's restaurant, who were urging me on from their fold-up lawn chairs as they drank beer. I felt sorry for them that they'd never know my tears.

CHAPTER 10

LAKE PLACID, MIRACLE...ON ICE

Let me start with issuing you a challenge: Be better
than you are. Set a goal that seems unattainable, and
when you reach that goal, set another one even higher.
                                          —Herb Brooks

A hundred-yard dash from the Wilderness Inn—and a sprinter would blow past me at the rate I was now slogging along on the bike—I came upon a large sign marking the entrance to Whiteface Mountain. This year, to give riders a fun respite from the grind of the Three Bears and rest of the last section of the bike course, planners added a new twist: a little loop through Whiteface.

Whiteface Mountain is the fifth highest mountain in New York and one of the High Peaks of the Adirondack Mountains. It was the site of the alpine events in the 1980 Winter Olympics, including the prestigious men's and women's downhill.

Many reminders of the 1980 Olympics remained on the mountain until the summer of 2019, when Whiteface Mountain management updated all the signs and took down the Olympic ones, including the Olympic scoreboard that had stood near the finish line where 1980 Olympians crossed.

Skiers can still ski the famous men's and women's downhill courses and see how they compare to the young Austrians who found gold hitting speeds close to 100 mph—or 60 mph faster than I had biked down the Keene descent that terrified me.

I suppose snow is a softer landing than pavement, but kissing trees on skis has proven to be an affair that only those listening to the eulogy of the departed tree-hugger will remember. In any event, good thing I wasn't reared as a downhill ski racer. It would have been a short career, most likely ended by an oak.

The legacy of the Olympics infuses the feel and fabric of everything in Lake Placid. The small Adirondack village has hosted two winter Olympics—in 1932 and in 1980—and you'd be hard-pressed to pass any shop on Main Street without a reminder, from Zig Zags Pub's bobsled on the sidewalk that every passing tourist stops to sit in for a photo to the Team USA hockey jerseys, tee shirts, and hats with the 1980 Olympic logo that line the shelves of all the stores.

I wanted to learn more about this charming village and the history of the Olympics, so I convinced Jim to go to the Olympic Museum with me on Saturday afternoon between racking my bike for the race and carbo loading at Main Street Pizza. The museum is situated right in the center of town, up the hill from Ironman Village, and is not only a treasure trove of Olympic memorabilia, but also a fascinating look into the history of Lake Placid.

The first thing I came upon was a display about Dr. Melvil Dewey. I learned that Dewey not only created the Dewey Decimal Classification System; he also founded the Lake Placid Club in 1895, sparking the transformation that turned the sleepy town into America's premier summer resort. Members of the club saw how successful the summer outdoor recreation activities were, and in 1904–1905, they kept the club open in the winter.

The local citizens found the snow and ice and frosty air invigorating. I don't understand this at all, because I find snow and ice and frosty air...cold. But the hardy townies told their friends, word spread, and Lake Placid became a winter destination as well.

Other things the local community found invigorating were competitions and winter thrills, which, at the time, were few and far between. They craved strenuous activities. Well, no shit—they needed to find some way to keep warm. One man filled the void.

Henry Uihlein II, whose grandfather was a longtime president of the Joseph Schlitz Brewing Company, was attending college in New York City when he became afflicted with tuberculosis. He came to Lake Placid to treat it. The climate and altitude agreed with him, and the treatment was successful.

Restored to health, Henry rejoiced and poured his new-found energies into the burgeoning winter recreation scene. His passion was speed skating, and he resolved to make Lake Placid the greatest skating center in the United States.

His efforts led to Lake Placid securing its first international sanctioned event, the International Outdoor Speed Skating Championships. The small village of about 3,000 residents was now on the global winter sports map. As a result, Lake Placid was awarded the 1932 Winter Olympic Games, where Uihlein was an official timekeeper. (He also was an honorary member of the 1980 Winter Olympics, and one of the few individuals to be involved in both Olympics.)

"Wow! It says here that that old buzzard lived to 101 years old," I said to Jim. "I may have to reconsider my aversion to frosty air."

"Oh, please. You'd pick tuberculosis and a warm hospital bed over getting your little footsies cold in the snow," Jim said. "Pansy."

After reading about how this tiny town tucked away in the Adirondack Mountains in upstate New York became a summer and winter sports mecca, I came upon a section that examined what it takes to be an Olympian.

The display begins with this statement, next to a photo of Olympic speed skating gold medalist Apolo Ohno:

The Olympic Games have long challenged an
athlete's ability to balance body, mind, and spirit.
Achieving this balance can lead to greatness. To
do so, it requires endless repetition in training,
mental and physical; discipline; and passion.

"So does Ironman," I said. "But my experience is that end-less repetition in training only leads to endless repetitive inju-ries, like stress fractures and rotator cuff tears."

"How the hell would you know?" Jim roared. "Your expe-rience? Endless repetition doesn't mean three swims in the pool the week before the race." He scowled at me. "Are you writing that down?" he asked as I scribbled in my Moleskine pad. "Don't bother. The only thing you're great at is having no discipline."

"One year I will, Jim. One year I'll go all-in like an Olympian."

"You've been saying that for ten years."

I didn't like this line of attack and turned back to the dis-play. As I gazed at Apolo Ohno, I became curious about the origin of his name, so I pulled out my phone and googled "Apollo." "It says here that the Greek god Apollo was the ideal of the kouros, which means he had a beardless, athletic, and youthful appearance."

"Which is the god that represents unkempt, slovenly, old, and broken down? That would be you," said Jim.

"I am Ares, god of war, and I'm going to kick your ass with my violent and untamed demeanor. And if we're picking gods, you'd be Dionysus, for the record," I said.

"Who is Dionysus?"

"God of wine."

"I'm not offended."

"You should be, you grape-curating drunk."

"If you're not careful, I'm going to make like Thor and drop the hammer on you."

"Thor is not a Greek god. Get your mythology right."

"Eat me. Oh, and by the way, Apolo Ohno wasn't named after Apollo the god."

"Who's he named after then?"

"It says here he was named after some Greek words that mean 'get out of the way' and 'look out, here he comes.'"

"Well that's stupid." Resigned to an unbalanced mediocre life, I moved on to the next quote, this one by Apolo himself:

> *"Bottom line is that you've trained 4–8 years of your life at a chance at a race that lasts 40 seconds long that is distinguished between a thousandths of a second, which is an eye blink, and that's the difference between 1st and 4th place."*

"Jim, look at this," I said, pointing to the quote. "Maybe we're not the stupid ones. Next time Karoline gives me grief about going for a long training ride, I'm going to say, 'Honey, what if you had married an Olympian? They train for four to eight years for a race that lasts forty seconds, where if they're an eye blink slower than the next guy, they get squadoosh! I train for four to eight months and get to savor my race for up to seventeen hours! That's great value!'"

"No, I think it's safe to say that we're the stupid ones," Jim said.

We continued walking through the display, reading the quotes that described what it takes to be an Olympian, and by simple extrapolation, an Ironman.

DISCIPLINE

Self-discipline is a trait needed for all athletes to accomplish their goals.... Temptations to veer away from their goals are numerous, but it takes discipline and a clear, conscious effort to maintain consistency and regularity, even on bad days.

"I know you want a large cheesesteak sub, a plate of fries, and an ice-cold beer right now," I said.

"The only temptation I have is to punch you in the face," Jim replied. "That's not true. I do want the cheesesteak. And the fries. And the beer. You asshole."

REPETITION

Athletes practice skills over and over, what seems like a million times during training…. By repeating certain training sets over time, athletes can improve motor skills, develop an intuitive understanding of their body, and ultimately be able to efficiently perform to the best of their capability on race day.

"I've developed an intuitive understanding of my body," Jim said. "Right now, it's telling me to find a hammock and a chocolate cake."

"Why do we do this?" I asked. "Why do we do Ironmans?"

"Why do people climb Everest?" Jim countered.

"Because they're willing to suffer and risk their lives to experience the exhilaration and exaltation of reaching the summit of the highest place on Earth?"

"Why did John Glenn go into space?" Jim continued. "Why did Jacques Cousteau dive deep under the sea? Why did Columbus sail to the New World? Why did Lindbergh fly around it alone? Why did that nutjob climb El Capitan with no ropes or harnesses?"

"Because they wanted to push boundaries, explore new frontiers, take risks, test their skill, do what nobody had done before, become immortal?"

"No," Jim said. "Because they were stupid."

CHAPTER 11

GOLDILOCKS AND THE THREE BEARS

When your legs scream stop and your lungs
are bursting, that's when it starts. That's the
hurt locker. Winners love it in there.
— Chris McCormack, Australian triathlete

Miles 51–53 (53.4–55.4)

I came to the infamous Three Bears. Actually, Goldilocks comes first, shortly after the fifty-mile marker. The Three Bears get all the attention, but in my opinion, Goldilocks is a close second to Papa Bear in difficulty. She deserves more respect. She's a subtle killer who will break your spirit and eat your soul—a tough, if unheralded, young broad.

After Goldie, in quick succession come Mama, Baby, and Papa. Mama is a grind. Baby Bear comes immediately after Mama and is quite harmless. Not much of a hill, really. Then you meet Papa. He's a beast. Now, I'm not saying Papa Bear is Mount Everest or anything. In the scheme of things, he's not a very steep or long hill, much the same way the famous Heartbreak Hill from the Boston Marathon in and of itself is not an Olympus, but it still rips the heart out of thousands of runners every year.

It's all in the placement. Heartbreak Hill comes after the twentieth mile of the marathon, when legs are rubbery and the tank is nearly empty. Goldilocks and the bears come at the end of each loop, one after another. What would be a relatively easy climb at mile ten, after fifty and one hundred miles is a battle against Thanos after he has all the infinity stones. An unfair fight.

TIP: Stay relaxed on the bike. Keep your shoulders and neck as loose as possible. Just relax. If you tense up, the second half of the bike will be brutal.

I started up Goldilocks and remembered the story about five-time Tour de France winner Jacques Anquetil. He used to put his water bottle in his shirt instead of on the bike during climbs. Thought it made the bike lighter. He had complete faith that it worked and that it made his climbs easier.

Ironman participants all have our faiths we cling to. One of mine was the Mission EnduraCool cooling towel that I bought at Lowe's for $11.99. I saw an ad for it that touted how it had a patented cooling design that activated when it was soaked with water. *Cools to thirty degrees below the average body temperature! Absorbs sweat and moisture!*

I first deployed my magic towel for Ironman Boulder in 2014. While Jim and all my other competitors were broiling in the hot sun, I'd be cool as a Henry Uihlein II filling his lungs with frigid air. I was convinced this little blue rag was my secret weapon and mine alone—the edge to give me my PR, or my personal record finish.

Others could have $12,000 bikes tested in wind tunnels and crafted to capture every aerodynamic advantage. They could have the latest Zipp wheels. They could have $400 aero TT helmets. They could be doping, lined up in some secret medical facility hooked up to an IV, getting cheetah blood transfusions the morning of the race. I had a sweat rag from Lowes to keep me cool.

I followed my new voodoo religion blindly like a David Koresh follower right up until Janet Reno burned the church compound down. My conflagration happened on the bike, where my leg muscles burned out by mile eighty and my body melted in Boulder's summer heat.

That race also featured my dabbling with oxygen water. I learned about it when a woman stopped me in a Barnes & Noble in Valencia, California, one morning. I was wearing my 2012 Lake Placid Ironman finisher shirt. (I always wear my Ironman swag so people know I'm a bad mofo.) She said she was a nutritionist and worked with triathletes and told me about a new product she was selling that had worked wonders for her clients: water infused with extra oxygen—O-x-i-g-e-n.

Oxigen – enhanced with powerful O4 oxygen molecules that will give your whole system a lift…now you can instantly replenish and restore your brain, body, and spirit with every sip!

The woman said it would make my heart and muscles work more efficiently. She said it would give me more stamina. She said it would aid in a quicker recovery. She said if I used it, I would definitely beat Jim in Boulder. I immediately ordered a case of twenty-four bottles.

"You did what?" Jim asked. "You think drinking a bottle of oxygen water and wearing a sweat rag on your head is going to make up for the fact that you haven't trained? How about you try training for a change and see how that works?"

"I have trained," I said. "But this is just going to give me the edge I need to kick your ass in Boulder. You'll see."

"You're insane. Trust me, I can't wait to see your epic crash and burn as the Kane train comes rumbling by you."

Jim didn't have to wait long. I had my worst race ever in Boulder. I knew I was in trouble when I was gassed on the bike at about mile fifteen. I walked much of the run and finished in fourteen hours—more than thirty minutes after Jim. When I arrived back home, I used the rest of the bottles to water the plants. Maybe the oxygen would help them. And I turned my sweat rag into a car buffer, for which it was much better suited.

Perhaps this was harsh. Perhaps Jim was right and that my training and nutrition plan for Boulder had more to do with my subpar showing. Nevertheless, once you lose faith in something, it's hard to restore it. The only habit that carried over from Boulder to my current race was shaving my arms and legs to be more aerodynamic. If it didn't do much for me, that was okay, because it didn't cost much, and the hair grew back.

I do continually try new things, sometimes—like the pepper shot—without enough research and field testing, and to my detriment. This current race featured another product that I was trying out in an Ironman for the first time, something called Shroom Tech Sport from a company called Onnit.

A cyclist coworker of mine first introduced me to it. He said it gave him more energy during long rides. I was intrigued and looked it up. A main ingredient is cordyceps sinensis, derived from mushrooms that have been shown to help fight fatigue.

Here's how Onnit tells it:

> *Several thousand years ago high in the mountains of Tibet, herdsmen noticed that when their herds grazed on caterpillar fungus, they were noticeably more lively, energetic, and could stay on the move for far longer. Taking a lesson from their animal kin, they sampled the mushroom and found a similar effect. Unbeknownst to them were the mechanisms of action behind this highly prized*

mushroom. Containing the active ingredients adenosine and cordycepic acid, as well as a host of phytonutrients, cordyceps has been shown in some studies to increase oxygen utilization, aerobic capacity, and cellular energy.

They had me at caterpillar fungus. And who wouldn't want the endurance and energy of a Tibetan sheep? I ordered a bottle right away and tested it for a few long rides—taking four capsules precisely forty-five minutes prior to exercise as prescribed.

And…it worked. At least I think it did. I felt stronger than I had prior to using Shroom Tech Sport. I had more stamina at the end of long bike rides and runs. I was a convert. I read later on a sports nutrition site that cordyceps mushrooms also soak up stress and keep testosterone flowing. I had found my new religion.

Now, as I grinded up Papa Bear, I prayed that it would kick in, because I was gassed. I made exceptions for Shroom Tech that I hadn't for the Mission EnduraCool towel and Oxigen water. It wasn't Shroom Tech's fault that I did a pepper shot or ate too much undigestible food or crashed. Those were my errors.

Nor, I believed, could Shroom Tech be held responsible for my hamstring, quads, glutes, calves, and feet all cramping with a vengeance. But if I was going to finish this race, I needed a burst to kick in.

TIP: One investment that won't cost you much money but is critical to finishing an Ironman is a jar of Vaseline. Spread it generously on your undercarriage and nipples. You're welcome. On a related note, buy a bike seat that has a hole or cut-out in the middle. This is to relieve pressure. Your balls need a place to go when you're in aero.

Miles 53–56. (55.4–58.4)

I reached the top of Papa Bear, gasping and digging for... anything. Then I turned right onto Northwood Road, where another uphill climb greeted me. My feet were killing me. They needed to be stretched. It was the same pain you feel when wearing ice skates for the first time after a long period off. Your feet get fatigued.

Finally, a downhill. I stood on the pedals, glided, and stretched. Like a good morning stretch when you first awaken, it felt fantastic. I shook out my arms and legs. I turned down Mirror Lake Drive, where the crowds were loud and boisterous, a nice boost. I passed Jim and the guys cheering wildly. Then I came to my aunt's tent. I stopped.

TIP: Arrive a week before the race and stake out a good location for your family to watch. Set up a canopy/tailgate tent with comfortable chairs and lots of snacks and drinks. At Lake Placid, the best spot is on Mirror Lake Drive, close to the Lake Placid Pub & Brewery. That is in the heart of the action, walking distance to all the shops and restaurants, close to the swimmers' entry and exit, and right at the end of the biking and running loop.

Aunt Connie is one of those unheralded stars of the Ironman circuit. One often hears about the importance of preparation to achieving a successful outcome in the race. I admire those—like Jim—who have thought of every detail and covered every angle and are prepared for any and every surprise.

These are the people who have spares for their spares; who bring their Bullet blenders and spend each evening measuring the exact proportion of chia seeds, brussels sprouts, and protein powder they'll put in it; who know the temperature of the lake and the air and the humidity and wind intensity and direction it will be blowing so well you'd think they're preparing to be a meteorologist.

While athletes who prepare well are admired and sought after for advice (and often become coaches), spouses who plan and prepare the logistics of a family's role in a race don't get enough credit, much like an offensive lineman toiling anonymously in the trenches protecting the Tom Bradys who get all the accolades and attention.

Aunt Connie is a preparation ninja, a six sigma-level practitioner of Ironman logistics. Uncle Bob couldn't do what he does without her. She has the Ironman experience dialed in—

especially the Lake Placid experience. She rents the house, sets up the viewing tent, maps out the dinners, the beach time with the kids, where to park, the Dip 'n' Dash triathlon for the kids, knows the schedule of every exhibit and event in the Lake Placid and surrounding areas, prepares the meals, shops for mementos for the grandkids, and generally keeps everything running so Bob can focus on the race.

At this point, Bob has done so many Ironmans that he has lost track, but the number is well over fifty. And Connie has been there for almost all of them. She's supported him at Lake Placid for sixteen consecutive years. She knows that town and what happens during Ironman week so well that she could simultaneously run the town's visitor center and Ironman Lake Placid logistics.

Lucky for me, Karoline is also an organizer, so by the time I do fifty Ironmans, she'll also have everything locked in.

TIP: Find an Aunt Connie. Whether it's your spouse, your brother, your parents, your cousin, or a friend, they are indispensable.

"How are you feeling?" Connie asked.

"Do you have a motor I could borrow to attach to the bike for the second loop?" I asked. "How's Uncle Bob?"

"Oh, he's behind you a bit. But he's plugging along."

"I'll see you in a couple hours," I said. I took a sip of Gatorade and started up again with an effort much like the exertion required to start up a creaky fifteen-year-old lawn mower for the first time in spring. I turned onto Main Street and then passed the Herb Brooks National Hockey Center. I had finished...the first loop.

CHAPTER 12

I HAVE TO DO IT AGAIN??
ARE YOU $&%^#! KIDDING ME?

yes I said yes I will Yes.

— James Joyce

Miles 56–112 (59.4–114.4)

Why do I do this I can't feel my balls I think I shit myself I hate this fifty-six more miles of this torture she has a nice bum I'll follow her for a while good motivation slow down don't crash on Colden good crowd today in town supporting us they have a long day too do I have enough gels stomach feels a little better thank God there are the ski jumps I can't believe people ski off those hundreds of feet in the air nerves of steel I'm starting to chafe slow down miss nice bum I can't keep up with you now where will I find a spark horse stables Olympic ceremonies focus of the world at that time now just a forgotten field with a plaque and an unlit torch Olympic hockey team's motivation was beat the Soviets and become legends athletic pinnacle I will finish unknown and unloved athletic base camp stopped raining feet still soaked hope the Keene descent is dry

Dwayne crashed his bike in Aspen going down a hill in a race and woke up who knows how many minutes (hours?) later and continued the race that's nuts before concussion protocols I guess just like my Burbank crash woke up in an ambulance where is my bike I was more worried about what happened to my bike than the fact that I was in an ambulance I hope Joffrey has a bitter and painful death he deserves to suffer Cersei too she should have to be on this bike not me here comes white-knuckle time I'm Eddy the Eagle but without the crash at the end I hope these riders blowing past me are crazy why are they peddling for thirty seconds' gain it is nice to be able to just coast for a few miles my legs need a break okay coming to the end that wasn't too bad now just go at a good steady clip on the flats don't use up too much energy when did I take my last gel an hour ago it's time for another take a sip of water not too much well hydrated weird that you can become over hydrated there's a word for it I can't remember hypoxia or hyper-something I miss Karoline and the kids I wonder what they're doing today is it strange that they are vacationing at the Cape with my family without me I hope Peter and Fintan are giving Mimi lots of snuggles and that she is getting to spend some time with Nora they'll be swimming on the beach Peter is getting pretty good at it Fintan is still scared need to work with him maybe they'll train with me when they're older do an Ironman themselves I'd be reading a book on the beach right now drinking a gin and tonic but no I prefer to

suffer on this wretched bike my hamstrings feel like they're
going to snap need to work on Peter's reading I don't know if
he's in line with his class but it feels like he needs work Nora
loves the ocean she is not a baby anymore she's a full toddler
running around climbing up the dining room table I could
have brought them here but then it would have cost a lot more
I'd have to get a house in town and I wouldn't have been able
to focus though last time they had a blast wish Peter wasn't
scared to do the kid's run next time I'll make him and soon he
can do the dip and dash Fintan would do the run if Peter did
it with him he can run all day and does the Billy Goat trails
no problem next time I'll take them to the North Pole and
Santa's Village and Saranac and find a babysitter to watch the
kids and take Karoline for a romantic dinner at Lake Placid
Lodge that place looks gorgeous old money Gilded Age the
type of place F. Scott Fitzgerald would write about expensive
though god I hate my job I wish I could find something I like
better and make more money would be nice if I could work
for New Balance or Cervelo or make videos of the kids like
the Christmas jammies family who are they again ah yes the
Holderness or Dan Markham and What's Inside and travel
the world we could live anywhere spend some time in Europe
maybe Ireland so we wouldn't have the language barrier I loved
walking the bog in Cloonark quiet mossy fields my thighs are
scraping and scratchy need to make an adjustment should
have used more Vaseline down there about twenty miles left

oh lord I want to just get off this bike my feet are starting to go numb I need to shake them out I should get off the bike and stretch and take the shoes off and rub the blood back into my feet but I'm not going to do that I'll keep going and get to the run I can stretch in the tent what's my pace 14 mph slow and it's only going to get slower and I thought I'd do the bike in under six hours I'll be lucky if I can do it in seven that sucks there's Wilderness Inn take another gel and a few sips of Gatorade okay feeling like I always do at this point which is sore and tired and running out of gas the run will be a relief just to do something different that bastard keeps passing me and then I pass him we've been trading positions for forty miles no way I'm letting him pass again maybe not I don't have the strength anymore wow she does not look like an Ironman she may blow by me on the bike but I'll catch her on the run these fucking hills this is so beautiful with the river and the mountains alongside but hell would look better to me if I could get off this godforsaken bike there's the gorge where we went swimming yesterday washed down the rapids the pebbles and rocks ripped my stomach like a cheese grater Jim told me not to go near the rapids but I didn't listen now stomach is shredded up like I needed more adversity here's Goldilocks now Mama Bear oh god my legs and back I can't wait to get to the massage table I'll need to sit in a bucket of ice too and now Baby Bear this didn't seem bad on the practice ride Thursday awful now what's my pace 8 mph 8 pathetic mph can I do more no this is all I have hopeless okay Papa Bear ugh I never want to see a bike again almost there Jim and the guys will be at the lake yelling and screaming I'll go faster then just knowing the bike is done there they are still drinking lucky bastards they are great friends coming here to support me and cheer okay finally pulling into the oval don't crash during the dismount thank God this is over now the run let's not make this transition a Catholic service in and out survive and advance let's go!!!!

I can hear readers saying, *That bike ride sounds almost as long and tedious as that sentence he just wrote.*

The mind wanders during a 112-mile bike race.

CHAPTER 13
BREAKING DAWN. BREAKING BAD. BREAKING DOWN—TRAINING

We talking about practice. Not a game. We talking about practice…We ain't talking about the game, the actual game when it matters. We talking about practice.
— Allen Iverson

My chapter on training—if you listen to Jim—should read like one of those *Choose Your Own Adventure* books popular in the 1980s, where readers could make plot choices that determined the outcome of the story. *If you don't train properly, like Russ, proceed to any chapter named "Agony" or "Disaster" or some title that will accurately describe how race day is going to go for you. If you plan on training, like Jim, continue here.*

He told me that my chapter on training and preparation should just be a blank page. Fuck you, Jim! While that would be an easier chapter to write, I do in fact train, and I'd like to share a few thoughts on it.

If you really want to know what Ironman training is like, it's a pregnancy: nine months of discomfort, nausea, soreness, and wild mood swings. But the result is well worth it. Unless you are the carrier of Satan's spawn and deliver Rosemary's Baby on the big day. Then it's just nine months of suck followed by depression and second-guessing that night you spent with a guy who called himself Beelzebub.

Finding time and motivation to train can be difficult. With three kids under the age of five, I feel guilty every time I tell them I can't play in the yard with them or read books or snuggle because I'm leaving for a long run or ride. I like being with my children (most of the time), and I rank snuggles far ahead of swimming endless, mind-numbing laps at the YMCA.

Yet I know that if I don't put in the time, I'll get killed on race day. It's a high-wire act that requires commitment and some creativity. And money. And a forgiving spouse. Not necessarily in that order.

You can't half-ass training for an Ironman. You can get by in a sprint tri or Olympic-distance tri if you haven't put in the hours and miles. But if you think you can do an Ironman without putting in the time, you're going to do about as well as a Kardashian dropped into the wilderness with Bear Grylls. So I had to put in the time, as best I could, meaning I'd tick Karoline off every week and have a bad case of Irish guilt for a couple of months.

My first brush with guilt was when I attempted to begin my training program in January of 2018—a solid six months before the race. I was like the Pillsbury Doughboy after a long winter's hibernation from exercise, and I needed to at least get the body used to the shock of moving around again.

"I think I'm just trying to pile on additional challenges by getting in the worst possible shape before the Rocky music comes on and I turn it around," I told Jim.

"Heighten the dramatic impact, right? That's my story."

"The problem is, the Rocky music for you usually doesn't come on until June," Jim said. "When everyone else is tapering, you're ramping up."

"Baseless lies," I said.

"Have you started training yet?" Jim asked.

"I climbed the stairs at work instead of taking the elevator. That's a start."

"You're a clown."

I called him back that night. "I'm going to start training tomorrow. This will be the earliest I've ever started preparing for an Ironman. I'm going to really do it this time."

"Here we go again," he said. "We all know your training program is a soft launch.

You'll test it out for a day or two and then sit on your ass for a month."

"Not this time. I built in a foolproof plan to make sure I stay the course: I just signed up for the Ironman 70.3 Eagleman early June. So now I have an undercard race motivating me nearly two months before the main event. And I can use Maryland to measure my progress."

"I'm calling bullshit," Jim said. "It's fifteen degrees out. You're a scared little groundhog who pops out of his hole, and if it's below sixty degrees outside, you turn around and burrow back into your bed until summer. There is no way you are going to train properly for a race in early June."

"I'll show you. If this groundhog sees his shadow, he's going to shadowbox it and pretend he's punching your ample gut."

I called Jim that night. "I may have had delusions of grandeur when I spoke with you earlier."

"I'm so surprised."

"I bundled up and planned to run about three miles. I got a hundred yards and shut it down. I folded laundry instead, and it wiped me out. I ended up sitting on the couch watching about two hours of *Everybody Loves Raymond* reruns."

"What did I tell you? You're soft."

"If I'm being honest, sometimes I wish I was a nursing mother."

"What the hell are you talking about?"

"I read that exercise breast milk doesn't taste good because it contains large amounts of lactic acid, making it sour," I said.

"Your point?"

"If I were a nursing mom, I'd have a built-in excuse not to run. *Sorry, I can't run for the next six months. I don't want the baby to drink sour breast milk.*"

"You're hopeless."

Jim was right about one thing: I *was* soft. A run outside in January or February was fraught for me. First, I hate running in the cold. Second, I hate running in the cold. While Jim regularly banged out fifteen-mile runs in the New England snow, I stayed inside, huddled by the fire, wishing for a warm spell that wasn't coming.

The idea of hopping into any body of water in the winter when it's still freezing outside is not something I particularly enjoy. Unless the body of water is housed within a jacuzzi and has a built-in cup holder for a beer. Of course, biking outside in winter was also completely out of the question.

To get some initial aerobic work in, I started getting up early in the morning to ride my Sunny stationary bike down in the basement before the kids woke up. Despite starting at 5 a.m., I was lucky if I got fifteen minutes into it before one of the kids appeared and wanted something to eat or a glass of water, or I heard one of them crying and had to end my workout to snuggle them back to sleep.

The kids had an uncanny sense of when I was up. No matter how early I rose, they'd get up too and ruin my workout. If I set my alarm for 5 a.m., Fintan would roll down just as I started pedaling the stationary bike. If I got up at 4 a.m., Nora would jump on my back as I began a set of push-ups. It was impossible, and I realized I needed to move my workouts off campus.

So I signed up for a VeloLabs twelve-week winter training session at my local bike shop, Green Lizard Cycling in Herndon, Virginia. This is where the guilt kicked in.

Green Lizard is a hip, locally owned bike shop right off the Old Dominion bike trail. Not only do they sell a wide selection of bikes and have excellent mechanics who fix them quickly at reasonable rates, but they also function as a café and serve coffee, baked goods, soups, sandwiches, and an expansive list of beers—on tap or in a can. They have established a friendly, community atmosphere.

My VeloLab sessions were Wednesday evenings at 6:30 p.m. I walked into my first one ten minutes late because I thought I had enough time to stop home after work and wolf down a quick dinner. That was dumb. As I wheeled my bike through Green Lizard's café area, a reception of jolly patrons laughed and drank and watched me with pity. I continued past the revelry to the back of the house, where serious cyclists were already spinning furiously.

Matt Pickworth, the fit and friendly manager of the program, set my bike up in front of a wall of screens worthy of NASA, flashing a jumble of data indecipherable to me at that moment. He hooked up a cadence sensor and power meter to my bike so my data would be displayed on the screen.

"Do you know your max threshold power?" he asked.

I didn't have a clue. I looked to my left at a woman in her mid-to-late fifties who couldn't have weighed more than a hundred pounds. "A little more than hers," I said.

While I pedaled and sweated up and down simulated hills at the back of the shop, beer and laughter flowed from the lively social gathering in the front. Perhaps it was some sort of sick Ironman preparation set up by VeloLabs; we killed ourselves while wiser people enjoyed their Golden Helles Lagers and watched us kill ourselves. Just like Ironman race day.

That first session featured a twenty-minute functional threshold power test.

I watched my wattage and cadence on the wall in front of me. In fact, I could watch everyone's. During my test, my wattage, or the amount of power I was generating, averaged 168 watts, reaching a maximum output of 318 watts. That wouldn't power a toaster. My average cadence, which measures revolutions per minute (RPMs) was 96, with a max of 111. My average speed was 19.04 mph.

That all was fine with me until I saw that the AARP waif had better numbers. I had some work to do.

The eleven 65–70-minute subsequent workouts were designed to incrementally push me further aerobically and increase my sustainable power, help me climb better, and improve my overall cycling performance.

Unfortunately, the sessions occurred right in the middle of dinner and stretched through the kid's bedtime. So on

Wednesday evenings, Karoline got stuck preparing and refereeing dinner, nursing Nora and putting her to bed, and then wrestling the boys to get their jammies on, read the bedtime stories, and threaten and cajole them for forty-five minutes to try to get them to stay in their beds.

Karoline was okay with it, but I felt bad about sticking her with those nighttime duties. It also turned out to be difficult to make it to the Green Lizard in time. As a result, I ended up attending only three sessions. The last one, in March, was a disaster. I ate a big meal right before getting on the bike and felt like I was going to throw up the entire time.

My numbers were worse than the first week, and I never made another session. More delusions of grandeur and $300 down the drain. I decided to just wait for the warmer temps, which didn't come until April. In the meantime, I began to think more creatively about how to multitask.

To make my balancing act work for my Lake Placid training, which would be the first attempt at training for an Ironman with three kids, I first needed to acquire a few items.

My mother, perhaps sensing an intervention was necessary to save a marriage, had already bought us the BOB Rambler jogging stroller with the twelve-inch air-filled tires and mountain bike-style suspension system. This was a big help…when we had only one toddler. I could plop Peter in, buckle him up, and run for hours around the paseos of Valencia when we lived in CA and I was training for Ironman Boulder.

Then Fintan arrived, and we had two toddlers. The BOB was still indispensable. I could take one of the boys and Karoline could wrangle the other. Then Nora came, and if I was going to sell six months of training to Karoline, I needed to be able to take two kids off her hands.

Thankfully, Karoline's friend—likely responding to a cry for help—gifted us her Baby Trend Expedition *double* jogging stroller. I could strap Nora and Fintan in and run until they got bored and asked to get out. It was a bonus if they fell asleep, which they did often. Built-in naptime! This act of generosity by me left Karoline with Peter, the most self-sufficient child, and no doubt good feelings toward her super helpful, most thoughtful spouse.

So I had the run covered, but what about the bike and swim? I needed to figure out a way to get more time in the saddle and in the pool. A little innovative thinking solved that problem. For the bike, as previously documented, I incorporated my training into my work commute. I could bike the twenty miles into DC faster than I could drive there in the Washington traffic anyway, so that worked out.

I also purchased a used Burley D'Lite X two-seat bike trailer on Craigslist for $100. These cost nearly $900 new. I hooked it up to my wife's bulky beach cruiser and pulled the kids around the neighborhood. You can get in some good hill work pulling two kids up a steep incline with a bike that weighs thirty pounds.

Then, in what I thought was a brilliant stroke, I signed the boys up for swim lessons at the YMCA. As they learned to blow bubbles and flutter kick in the good hands of the instructors, I would swim laps a few lanes over. There was one slight, wrinkle: as soon as Fintan learned that he was going in the water without his dad, he shrieked and screamed like a deranged banshee.

Turns out that he was deathly afraid of the pool. The instructor tried to pry him away, but she needed a better crowbar. He was not going to let go. So much for my plan. Stupid mistake. I should have signed up Peter alone. Luckily, swim training takes the least amount of time, at least for me, and I was able to carve out enough on the weekends to at least get my aerobic capacity to an acceptable level.

Overall, I had taken multitasking to the next level. I was quite proud of my ingenuity. Plus, pushing and hauling kids around when I ran and biked would make untethered running and biking seem like a breeze—like moving from a truck pulling a trailer up a hill to a turbo-charged Audi on the Autobahn.

Karoline would sing my praises to her friends. "Yeah, Russ is so helpful with the kids. He always takes them so I can go to lunch with friends and catch up on *Schitt's Creek*. He's so thoughtful."

Pleased with myself, I called Jim. "Jim, I should write a book about balancing family life with training for an Ironman. I'm like a Jedi Master."

"Jedi Master? More like a shuffling Jawa! Your book will be about as comprehensive as *Hop on Pop,* and it will be sold in the fantasy section."

"This coming from the guy whose nearest *Star Wars* comp is Jabba the Hutt," I said.

"Watch it."

Jim turned out to be right. My house of cards fell apart within a few weeks. The double stroller wobbled horribly when I got up to running speed. I got bored pulling the Burley up and down the hills of the surrounding neighborhoods. And I couldn't bear the guilt of Fintan's screams and ended up in the pool, holding him for the entirety of his lessons.

I found other options. I joined pick-up basketball games in the gym at work during lunch. In my mind, that covered my running requirements. If there wasn't a game, I'd hit the treadmill or elliptical and read a book. I also took Peter to the local ice rink on weekends and skated. A dozen or so sprints down the ice worked up a good sweat and got the heart pumping. It also strengthened my legs without putting the wear and tear on ligaments that running does.

TIP: Don't skimp on stretching. Take stretching as seriously as you do swimming, biking, and running.

I also did weight training. I had joined LA Fitness and hired a personal trainer when I lived in California, and he had given me a workout to do. I dug up the paper that the exercises were written on. He had told me it was nearly impossible, and he didn't think I'd be able to do it. He was right. Here's the workout:

50 burpees

50 pushups

50 jump squats

50 jump lunges

50 regular lunges

1 min. plank

50 scissors

50 leg raises

100 crunches

1 min. dying cockroach

REPEAT 5 TIMES

One set was more than enough for me. But I did that one set. Okay, I did half of it. A quarter. I did ten sit-ups a couple of times and held a plank for a few seconds. Someday I'd tackle it. But not any of those days leading up to Lake Placid.

I did, however, do P90X workouts once a week. That weight training was valuable in strengthening my core, building strength in my legs and arms, and speeding up my metabolism.

Jim mocked my unconventional approach, but I think mixing it up kept me from getting bored—and kept me out of the cold (okay, ice rinks are not exactly warm, but they are tolerable) until I felt motivated enough to get back in the pool, on the bike, and on the road.

The week before the Eagleman 70.3, I texted Jim. "Five days out from Maryland. Just finished a three-mile run. Feeling STRONG!"

He wrote back: "It's only three miles. Don't get cocky, dipshit."

I ended up doing fine at Eagleman. Even though I was fighting a cold, I finished in a respectable 5 hours and 43 minutes. But I was exhausted after, and the recurring thought in my head was, How the hell am I going to do double that in a few weeks?

Jim had started running too, preparing for Ironman Chattanooga, which would take place in September that year. "The Kane Train has left the station, but one awkward step on an acorn and this whole thing is derailed," he said. He had been dealing with a number of injuries, from a bum shoulder to ankle and back ailments. At this point, his body was being held together by duct tape and chicken wire.

"I'm as durable as IKEA furniture," he said.

"Worse," I said. "I think at this point you've got a particle-board body. It's liable to crumble into dust at any moment. I'm going to start calling you particle-board man."

One afternoon, he sent me an ominous note. "I think I need to shut it down," he said.

"Oh, stop whining, drop the chalupa and get back out there," I wrote back.

He called. "No joke, I went two miles and had to shut it down because the pain in my foot was so bad. I don't know if I can keep this pace. I had a pinewood derby car like this once—streaking to the finish only to have the wheels fall off."

"Maybe you'll finally listen to me," I said. "You never have to shut it down if you never start it up in the first place."

He laughed at that one. "Seriously, I keep trying to get faster, and my body keeps getting slower. The older I get, the more injuries I have, and the longer it takes to recover. I just don't know if I'm going to make it."

"Not me," I scoffed. "In fact, I should bring a camera with me to Lake Placid and film "Russ vs. Time" like Tom Brady."

"That's because you don't train. As soon as you do, time is going to kick your ass. I don't know if you want to film that," Jim said.

"I'm the lurking shark just watching you guys burn yourselves out and get injured. Like the Wicked Witch of the West, I'm just biding my time."

"You remember what happens to the witch. She ends up melting down into a puddle, just like you will at Lake Placid."

Jim's foot healed, and he resumed running the following week. Then he got hit by a car while on a training run and banged up his knee. "Are you going to get it looked at?" I asked.

"No, I'm going to open another bottle of wine and lie on the couch."

"That's a good attitude."

"This from the guy whose training program is a soft launch."

"What are you talking about? I did a one-mile swim this morning and then ran twenty miles," I said. "I'm hitting it hard!"

"Wow! Seriously? Good for you!"

"Thanks…. Okay, I exaggerated a little there. I just walked twenty feet to get a cookie, and I took a shower. But I did do two bricks over the weekend."

"Uh huh. Does that mean you took two craps this weekend?"

"Very funny."

"Okay then. What did you do? How many miles?"

"Well, I'm not sure of the miles, but I did a half-hour bike and a half-hour run on Saturday, and I did an hour bike on Sunday but had to cut the run short after twenty minutes because we had a birthday party."

"Are you doing a sprint tri?" Jim asked. "If you're training for a sprint tri, then you're doing great. Keep doing what you're doing. You do know that Lake Placid is an Ironman, right?"

"Don't worry. I've got three weeks," I said.

"I've heard enough. I'm going home to pour a glass of scotch and grab two bags of peas for my knees. Call me when you have some real training results to report."

Jim had another setback a few days later. This time, it was a mental, not physical, breakdown.

I had seen a news report that Caballo Blanco, the "White Horse," the distance-running legend featured in the bestselling book *Born to Run*, died from cardiomyopathy due to an enlarged heart while on a trail run, and I called Jim immediately. Caballo had been his hero. In fact, I had given Jim the nickname Caballo Rojo in homage, because he was built like a horse and had red hair.

"Jim! Caballo had a heart attack during a run and died! Do you believe it? He was the poster boy of stamina and strength, but they're saying all his running put too much stress on his heart."

There was silence on the other end of the phone as Jim processed this news.

"That's messed up," he said. "It makes no sense. I need to re-evaluate everything."

More silence.

"Jim? You there? What do you mean? What are you going to do?"

"Well, right now, I'm going to go out for ice cream sundaes with the kids. Then I plan to not move from the couch for four days. Based on the information you've given me, I don't think it's wise to overexert myself at this time."

"You need to do something," I said. "You can't just sit on the couch and calcify."

"I am doing something. I'm doing crunches two times a day."

"That's good, keeping your core strong for—"

"Cap'n Crunch in the morning, and Nestle's Crunch in the afternoon."

I offered that the *American Journal of Clinical Nutrition* states that running and other types of vigorous physical activity reduce a person's overall risk of a heart attack by as much as 50 percent, and that they are also less likely to suffer from strokes, diabetes, and other "lifestyle" diseases.

"Lifestyle, meaning sitting on the couch, watching SportsCenter, drinking beer, and eating nachos and cheesesteak subs?" Jim asked.

"Probably something like that," I said.

"I'll take my chances with that option."

CHAPTER 14
DROP THE CHALUPA— NUTRITION

Man is what he eats.
— Ludwig Feuerbach

Speaking of lifestyle choices and nutrition, while Jim was more disciplined than me in the training department, I had much more self-control when it came to eating right.

That wasn't always the case. In fact, my first step on the road to Lake Placid, before I even started training, had been to rein in my poor dining habits. By the end of December 2017, after a long sedentary holiday season filled with parties, glasses of wine, cookies, candies, and pies—and zero exercise—I was a doughy 146 pounds, which was eleven pounds over my typical race weight.

My three-year-old subsisted on PediaSure and Goldfish crackers and seemed to have boundless energy, so I thought for a moment about adopting his diet. Then I remembered that I'm a grown-up.

Instead, I hired a nutritionist to help me change my ways and slim down, and on a cold December day, like so many others who make resolutions at that time, I stepped into a CrossFit gym. But unlike all the others in the gym, I wasn't there to work out. I was there to meet Sarah Mills, founder of SoMoved Nutrition and a certified nutrition coach.

Sarah is an expert on nutrition, fitness, performance, and healthy lifestyles. In addition to a nutrition guru, she's also a kick-ass athlete and a CrossFit Level 3 trainer. I stepped into her small, windowless bunker at the CrossFit gym. A whiteboard with three columns and three words at the top of each column—carbs, protein, and fat—was perched in the corner. Each column contained lists of foods that fit under the corresponding header.

I had filled out an assessment form detailing my eating habits and goals, so she had an idea of the frog that she would try to turn into a prince. She told me to stand in the corner and take my shirt off for a photo session. These would be the "before" in the before-and-after photos.

She took my weight and measurements. Then she pulled out a scanner that looked like the early, bulky iPods and worked like the paddle gynecologists rolled around a woman's belly during ultrasounds, including the use of cold gel. It measured body fat percentage and muscle quality. She held it tightly against my quads, triceps, and abs until it registered a reading.

Here were my measurements on December 20, 2017:

Weight: 146

Waist: 34

Body Fat: 20.7 percent

Abs Fat: 38.4 percent

Muscle Quality: 46.7 percent

Lean Body Mass: 115.5

She told me I needed to eat clean, which meant limiting or eliminating processed foods. I also needed to measure my portions. I was supposed to send her a tracker each week with details of everything I had eaten and the precise portions. I was a horrible client. Jim, being the detail man that he is, would have thrived.

I, however, never measured anything. I just eyeballed everything. I was like a middle schooler with missing homework each week, and Sarah had to cajole and make do with the meager offerings of data I gave her.

Here's a typical e-mail from her:

> *Hi Russell,*
>
> *Been checking in on your tracking spreadsheet and see no updates! Shoot me a note on how you're doing!! And if possible, please post your progress on our tracker so we have some data for you!! I've forwarded this note through the tracker (Google Sheets) to share it with you again and be*

*sure you have access (have done that a few times
now). Let me know that you're okay getting into
the file with your plan and data!!*

And this, a few days later:

*Checking in again with you to see what you need
and how you're managing through the tracking
and eating! Let me know how I can help. Know
that the more info we have on how you're able to
do this, the more accurate our adjustments and
support for you will be. Good luck and let me
know how you're doing!*

Sarah

Poor Sarah. I was not giving her much to work with. But
I *was* listening. And while I wasn't one to measure and track, I
was doing the work. I cut out alcohol completely. I'm not a big
drinker to begin with, but I enjoy a glass of wine or two with
dinner. I stopped cold.

She told me to cut sweets and processed foods. Well...I
did not cut them completely, but I limited them. I had three
kids under five and a wife who loves to bake cookies and muffins and all sorts of sweets. Instead of eating two or three cookies, maybe I'd limit it to one.

At the office, I had to fight constantly the temptation of
slices of birthday cake offered at the seemingly weekly celebra-

tions, and the cookies or chocolates left out daily on the table in our hallway. Why were my coworkers constantly trying to sabotage me with sugar?

Lucky for me, Karoline is also a good cook, and she ensured that at least my dinners would be healthy and clean, with fish, lean meats, and lots of veggies like brussels sprouts, broccoli, and spinach.

And breakfast wasn't too bad. I started to read labels on cereal boxes and wouldn't buy any cereal with more than five grams of sugar. My go-to was Kix: three grams and still tasty. I added frozen blueberries to kick up the antioxidant-clean-eating factor a notch. More often than not, I made a protein smoothie with Simple Truth vanilla whey protein powder, almond milk, half a banana, frozen blueberries, spinach, beet powder, cinnamon, ginger, and flax and chia seeds.

But then there was lunch. I didn't have the time or energy to prepare healthy meals to bring to work. Sometimes I had leftovers from dinner, so I could maintain my clean eating. But too often I resorted to Philly cheesesteak subs from the food trucks. To feel good about myself, I'd also buy a side of brussels sprouts from Devon & Blakely, a little sandwich shop down the street from my office.

TIP: If you want to lose the love handles, boost your performance, and improve your overall well-being and day-to-day energy, cut out alcohol, processed ingredients, additives, sweeteners, and sugar.

Eat a more natural, whole food diet with a balance of lots of veggies, like broccoli, brussels sprouts, and spinach; good fats, like nuts, seeds, virgin olive oil, and coconut; and lean proteins, like chicken and fish.

Jim was not as successful. Part of it was that he was in sales and traveled a lot. Every time I spoke with him, he seemed to be at a drive-through or fast-food counter. He liked to eat. And drink.

"Hey, this clean eating is working," I told him. "I've cut down on sweets and cut out desserts and wine with dinner. Last night, I had a small piece of salmon, some broccoli roasted in olive oil, and a few fingerling potatoes. The weight is coming off, and my muscle quality is coming on strong!"

"Oh yeah, I just had a small meal last night too," he said. "Two cheeseburgers and a bucket of fries. But it's okay, because they were sweet potato. Then, for dinner, I ate an entire pizza."

"Are you trying to win fat bear week? Do you want me to start posting your photos online next to the bears so people can vote for you?"

Jim's meals came with names, like "The Cure," which consisted of a bacon cheeseburger topped with a fried chicken breast topped with a sunny-side egg. Hours after consuming it, writhing in agony and in need of a toilet, he renamed it "The Cause."

Another was the "UK Preflight Morning Crapper with a Pint." This was what looked like a meal for a family that he was consuming as a single individual. It was a massive plate full of scrambled eggs, sausage links, strips of bacon, baked beans, mushrooms, and fried tomatoes, plus a pint of Guinness... for strength!

Then there was the "Meatsweat Special," Jim's homemade beef Wellington wrapped in about a pound of prosciutto.

He sent me a photo of it and texted, "I must have eaten seven pounds of meat last night. Can only manage a short run today—five miles."

"Jim, you've got to stay the course! You'll never drop weight eating like that."

"I'm more focused on the main course."

"Well drop the chalupa and focus!"

Was I perfect in my diet? Far from it. I still couldn't totally resist the daily onslaught of baked goods at home and at work, foisted upon me by Karoline and my evil coworkers. But I made sacrifices and stuck to them, and six months later, on the eve of Ironman Lake Placid, I was shocked at the results.

TIP: Hire a nutritionist who routinely measures your progress. It can be an effective motivation tool because you'll see results, and you'll want to continue to post good numbers. You won't want to go for your check-in and be embarrassed that you gained weight and body fat. So you'll do whatever it takes—including a weekend at the sweat lodge—to hit your numbers.

I walked into Sarah's office in July feeling good. Her passion and enthusiasm for her clients' success was infectious, and I found myself wanting to do well for her, like a school student wanting to please the favorite teacher who has spent extra time on him because she sees potential.

I was anxious and excited to get my results. I had been steadily dropping weight and improving muscle quality, I had more energy and stamina, and I believed I was in the best shape I could possibly be for the upcoming race. Here were my measurements on July 3, 2018, a few weeks before Ironman Lake Placid:

> Weight: 130.6
> Waist: 29.5
> Body Fat: 13.4 percent
> Abs Fat: 13.2 percent
> Muscle Quality: 93.2 percent
> Lean Body Mass: 113.1

"You did awesome!" Sarah said. "You're going to do great at Lake Placid. You've got your plan, and you know what works for you. Just remember, don't introduce anything different on race day. Keep your routine the same. Eat the same things that have been working for you during training."

Boy, I was going to *kill* it at Placid.

CHAPTER 15
ICE BATHS AND BLACK & DECKER–RECOVERY

Old age ain't no place for sissies.
— Bette Davis

I hate ice baths. They're awful. That moment you first hit the water is like a thousand pinprick icicles poking your skin.

I finished what for me was my long training run of the season (twelve miles) and bought four bags of ice at 7-Eleven. I proceeded to dump those right into my bathtub, which was filled with cold water. Then I hopped in. My body started convulsing. After about ten minutes, I reached a Zen mode and became numb to it. Then I realized that my legs had actually gone numb. I couldn't feel them. Or my feet. I got out of the tub and nearly fell down, like I was newborn Bambi just learning to stand for the first time.

The numbness eventually gave way to a cold in my core that I couldn't shake. It was early July in Washington, DC, and eighty-eight degrees out, but I was wrapped in three layers—a tee shirt, pullover, and fleece—shivering like a Tongan lost in the Arctic.

It was a necessary evil. There are a lot of those when you get older, when you think you're still a springy young colt but you're a broken-down old cob. These days, it seems, I spend more time doing maintenance on the body—stretching, chiropractor visits, massage—than I do actually swimming, running, and biking.

As if I needed more proof of that new normal, the following week, after a sixty-mile bike ride, my back began spasming. I worried that this might derail my Ironman participation. Lake Placid was only a few weeks away.

I visited the first chiropractor I could make an appointment with, Dr. Jason Brown at Reston Healing Center. He started me with an hour-long deep tissue massage and then took X-rays. My spine was badly out of alignment—I could see my vertebrae pinching unnaturally.

Dr. Jason began cracking away, and after twenty minutes of popping that sounded like Peter eating Rice Krispies, he sent me on my way. I had two follow-up appointments before the race and did not experience any more muscle spasms. My back, if not my life, was properly aligned.

TIP: When your training gets more intense in the months prior to the race, go to a chiropractor once every two weeks for an adjustment and massage therapy. It's a little healthy gift to yourself.

I began to think more about how I could preserve my body as I journeyed through middle age. I remembered bumping into Herb Brown in 2016 while on a practice swim in Mirror Lake with Uncle Bob a few days before the race.

As Uncle Bob and I took off our wetsuits by the changing facility, we struck up a conversation with an elderly gentleman with an easy Southern drawl sitting on the stone wall. To my shock, he pulled a wetsuit and bathing cap out of his bag. He was also racing in the Ironman in the 80- to 84-year-old age group.

He was trying to learn whether a rival in his age group was racing, he told us. He hadn't seen him yet. His main concern was not surviving the race but rather beating this guy. "I'm going to kick his ass," he said. And then he laughed.

This guy started competing in Ironmans after he turned seventy-two and had participated in at least nine since then. I googled him and saw an interview where he said, "You use it or you lose it. I'm gonna use it." That's exactly what he also told us on the beach. I decided that I wanted to be like Herb, doing Ironman races when I'm eighty.

After some serious Google searches on how to stave off decay and decline, I started to seek out foods that countered that silent and secret killer: inflammation. My smoothies became jugs of free-radical-sucking goodness, filled with every possible anti-inflammatory ingredient—blueberries, black-berries, cherries, ginger, cinnamon, turmeric, cocoa powder, beet powder, spinach, and broccoli. I drank four cups of green tea a day.

I cut out all those evil foods that I adored so much that caused inflammation—sugar, white bread, MSG, soda, processed meats, cookies, ice cream, beer, and wine. Well, cut down, if I'm being honest. I'm not a Tibetan monk.

I also started stretching, something I hadn't done since high school soccer when the coach made us do it before practice. It was a revelation when my trainer at LA Fitness started stretching me out after workouts. One session, he had me lie on my back, and he lifted my leg up and pushed it toward my chest to stretch the IT band. I didn't even know what the IT band was, but when he stretched it, it hurt like a mother. But a good hurt.

I dusted off some yoga and stretching DVDs—Bryan Kest Power Yoga, P90X X Stretch, and New York City Ballet Workout. I hadn't realized how tight I was. My back, neck, hamstrings, and quads were guitar strings in danger of snapping the moment I strummed my first power chord.

I must admit, it was a challenge to find uninterrupted stretching time at home. It seemed anytime I was in the middle of a downward dog, my three kids saw it as a perfect opportunity to jump on my back and ride me like a mule. When I was in warrior or tree pose, they pulled a crouching tiger, hidden three-year-old leap from the couch and knocked me over. And then they giggled uncontrollably.

I had another revelation when we arrived in Lake Placid and settled into our room. Jim pulled out a knobby orange stick that he started rolling on his quad. "Are you making pie?" I asked. "What is that?"

"Mmm. Pie. That's not a bad idea. But this is a muscle roller."

"Can I try it?" I took the twenty-one-inch long orange stick—the TriggerPoint GRID STK Handheld Foam Roller—and started rolling it along my own quad. It was almost a sexual experience. I could feel the knots dissolving from my muscles.

It was designed to replicate the pressure of a massage therapist's thumb and channel blood and oxygen directly to muscle tissue. I held onto that beautiful orange stick for the next hour and just grinded away until I had worked out all the tightness and tension.

I knew I needed one of my own, so I ordered it on Amazon that night. And this incredible piece of knobby rubber that I would prize like Nora cherishes her dolls only cost $31.95.

While my stick and stretching and anti-inflammatory foods helped, I was always searching for other tools to help my creaky body survive another Ironman season. Through the years, I had begun to notice an increase in vendors in the athletes' village peddling products to promote recovery. This year, I decided to spend some time testing them out on Saturday afternoon after racking my bike.

I started at NormaTec (*The Ultimate Recovery Experience!*) where an inviting chair—a reclining, lounging lawn chair—beckoned me. A young hipster salesman told me to lie down, and then he put on what looked like two giant air casts and pulled them up to my waist. He connected a couple of hoses and turned a nob and the air casts compressed around my legs. The compression rolled slowly up and down, moving from ankles to quads and hamstrings and back again.

It felt a little like when you get your blood pressure taken at the doctor's office. I'd say it felt like a python constricting around my legs, but I've never experienced that, so I don't know exactly what it feels like. But I'd like to think it feels like a NormaTec boot, minus the death by asphyxiation.

NormaTec claims that this patented dynamic compression system increases circulation, reduces pain and soreness, rejuvenates muscles, and accelerates recovery. I can't vouch for these claims, but what I can say is my legs felt refreshed and rejuvenated after a twenty-minute session. And I felt as relaxed as if I had smoked a bag of weed while listening to Bob Marley on a beach in Hawaii.

This would be a great addition to my Ironman gear, I thought. I asked what it cost: $1,195. Maybe not. Karoline would kill me. Next booth.

The next item on *The Price Is Wrong* was an Aquilo portable cooling and compression system—cryo-compression. This was essentially a portable ice bath, in the form of compression pants that circulated ice water through a system of little bubbles that resembled bubble wrap woven into them. The salesman filled a little cooler with ice cubes and hooked up a tube to my pants, and ice water started rapidly flowing all around my legs.

As I luxuriated in freezing cold compression for the next twenty minutes, he told me that this system reduced muscle damage and pain, increased power, and improved sleep. Improved sleep!!?? Maybe it would watch over my kids at night and keep them from coming into my room and waking me up every ten minutes.

"LeBron James is a big fan of this system," the guy added casually.

"How much?" I asked.

"You get the entire system for $2,200," he said. A breakfast diner tip for LeBron James, but a mortgage payment for me. As much as I loved the Aquilo ice bath, for now I'd stick to the $6.85 it cost me to drop four bags of ice in my bathtub and suffer the numb legs. I continued on.

I came to a booth featuring a machine that looked like a fancy nail gun. It was a gun alright—a Theragun. I learned that the Pro-level model features two speeds: Kangaroo blunt force kick and jackhammer. Actual speed settings are 40 percussions per second (PPS) and 29 PPS. And what they call "treatment impact" is a max force of sixty pounds. To seal the sale, it also has an adjustable arm and an ergonomic multi-grip.

The way you used it was to turn the gun on and then "float" it along your muscles, lingering over tension trouble spots for no more than a few minutes. It's kind of like a high-speed meat tenderizer. You could use your Theragun prior to a workout, the saleswoman said, with a thirty-second session to activate or "wake up" your muscles, and then float your Theragun over sore muscles for a few minutes after a workout to decrease aches and discomfort.

"How much?" I asked.

"The G3PRO is $599," she said. "You can finance it," she added helpfully.

"I'll think about it. Thank you." Next. I'd just let Peter and Fintan punch me repeatedly in any sore muscle spots for free. I didn't need a Theragun as long as I had them.

TIP: If you're looking for a cheaper alternative to the high-priced recovery gadgets, go to Home Depot or Amazon and buy the Black & Decker WP900 Random Orbit Waxer/Polisher. It is a power waxer designed for cars and boats that works shockingly well as a hand-held massager. It spins and vibrates up to 4,400 orbits per minute and works out muscle tension every bit as well as any of the tools actually designed for that purpose. For $28.69, you can have a tool to warm up your muscles before a run or loosen them up after. It could be the best training recovery investment you ever make.

The afternoon wore on. By this time, Jim had joined me. I came to the last tent and watched a guy place two electrodes on a woman's shoulders. He held a little portable box the size of a small iPhone and pressed a few buttons. The woman's neck started pulsing, and a look of such ecstasy came across her face that I thought she was about to have an orgasm.

The man motioned us over. "You want to try it?" he asked.

"If it will put that look on my face, yes," Jim said.

"What does it do?" I asked.

"Everything!" the man said. "You're going to feel incredible."

"But what does it do?" I asked again.

"What doesn't it do?" he countered. "It relaxes muscle spasms, increases blood circulation, relieves muscle tension, breaks up lactic acid, stimulates inactive muscle fiber, relieves pain, and speeds up recovery."

"How does it work?" Jim asked.

"You just hook up the electrodes, place the gel pads directly on the muscles, turn on the electronic muscle stimulator, and set your preference. It generates multiple therapeutic pulses that target deep tissue and relieve muscle tension. It's like getting a deep tissue massage. Do you have any areas that are sore or tight?" he asked me.

My neck and shoulders were tight, so he hooked two circular electrodes to the base of my neck and pressed a button. I felt a faint pulse. He pressed the button again, and the pulse increased. I could feel my muscles contracting. He pressed it again. Stronger pulse. It felt glorious.

He had placed the larger, rectangular electrodes on Jim's hamstrings. I could literally see Jim's muscles jump with every pulse.

"How much for this?" I asked.

"This is the XPD—our best seller," he said. "It normally retails for $399, but I'll give it to you for $250."

"That's a bit rich for me," I said.

He looked at Jim. "How about you?" he asked. "You want one for $250?"

"Make me a deal," Jim said. "What can you do for us if we both buy one?"

"How about $200 each?"

"How about $150?" Jim said.

We each walked away with the twelve-mode, bestselling, sore today, strong tomorrow HiDow XPD stimulator for $150.

That night, back at the Wilderness Inn, I asked Jim to place the electrodes on my neck for another stimulation session. "How does this work again?" I asked.

"Let me see this," he said, taking the little control box. He unknowingly put it on the highest possible voltage and then pressed the button. My head went full Beetlejuice, eyes bugging out and hair standing on end. My neck muscles contracted so hard, it made my shoulders and arms jerk up like they were attached to strings being yanked by a giant puppeteer.

"Turn it off!!" I screamed. "Turn it off!! You motherfucker!!

Jim and Mark began laughing uncontrollably. "I didn't know your head was going to pop off," Jim said as tears of unbridled mirth streamed down his face.

"You asshole! Are you trying to kill me? I'm not some fucking Frankenstein experiment here for your amusement." All the relaxation and recovery I had worked so hard to achieve during the day was wiped out, and hours before the biggest race of my life, I was as tense as a man taking a paternity test on *Dr. Phil.*

CHAPTER 16

RUN, RUSSELL, RUN

Run when you can, walk if you have to,
crawl if you must, just never give up.
— Dean Karnazes, ultrarunning legend

I staggered into T2—the second transition tent—where you go to puke and let some strange latex-gloved man slather Vaseline all over your nipples, shotgun a bottle of Gatorade, put on some sneakers, and start running.

Only 0.5 percent of the United States' population has run a marathon. Of that half percent, 99.9 percent of them start the marathon on fresh legs. Oh, there might be some light stretching and twenty-yard warm-up jogs involved before you tackle those 26.2 miles. But in an Ironman, you're already 114.4 miles in. I had a full marathon ahead of me, and I was already exhausted.

You have seventeen hours to complete the entire race. You start at 7 a.m., so the stroke of midnight is the cutoff. That's when your Cinderella story evaporates before your eyes and you turn into a distraught ball of unfulfilled pain, when you feel like you just ran twenty-six miles in glass high heels.

Of course, first you have to make the swim cutoff time—2 hours and 20 minutes—and swim and bike combined cutoff time—10 hours and 30 minutes. If you succeed in that, congratulations. Up next is a version of Navy SEALS Hell Week. You will now endure toenail trauma, a swelling brain, microscopic muscle tears, cardiac drift (a sharp spike in heart rate), blisters, chafing, liver overdrive, shin splints, and the equivalent of setting a jackhammer to your knees for five hours.

TIP: Wear compression socks and pants. Wear compression socks and pants. Wear compression socks and pants. Your calves and quads will thank you. Profusely.

Mile 1 (115.4)
Stupid me, who had ventured into this insanity three times already and knew exactly what was about to come, trudged out of the transition tent, turned left onto Main Street, where throngs of happy people who weren't running cheered me on, and settled into a plodding rhythm.

The first thing I understood was that I could ruin my run in the first 400 yards. Most of the first mile is a steep downhill. The crowds are dense, loud, and enthusiastic, and they provide a *Chariots of Fire*-worthy soundtrack of pump-up music to get you going.

I had seen runners get seduced by all this, go too fast, and take a header straight into the pavement, looking more like the competitors in the annual Cooper's Hill Cheese-Rolling race careening, cartwheeling, and crashing down the treacherous hill near Gloucester, England, while trying to catch a nine-pound block of cheese rolling down at speeds up to 70 mph.

A wipeout here by an overzealous runner trying to sprint down these first steep hills on exhausted, wobbly legs would most likely end his or her day. This would not be me. Not today. I couldn't have sprinted if there was a *Raiders of the Lost Ark* boulder made of cheese bearing down on me. Slow and steady was my initial pace, before just slow took over in the later miles.

TIP: Choose an initial pace that you know you can improve upon. For the first four to five miles, go slower than you think you should. You're starting a marathon seven hours into the event. Take time to settle in.

I was cautious going down that first big hill, but not so in other areas. Like selecting running shoes. In fact, I threw caution to the wind in my approach to footwear. In a shocking twist, I was trying out new shoes. Testing new shoes in a marathon is fraught with risk. Running works out 26 bones, 33 joints, 112 ligaments, and a network of tendons, nerves, and blood vessels...in the feet alone. You want to make sure those tootsies are as comfortable and well-supported as possible.

The smallest thread sticking out could cause friction over the course of five hours that would turn your foot to bloody hamburger. The slightest space at the toe could rip a toenail right off. A wrong fit could lead to blisters or plantar fasciitis. A shoe that didn't provide enough arch support could make your knees throb.

But to hell with the risks! I like a fresh pair of kicks for each race.

I have flat feet, so I always bought shoes that have good arch support, like Brooks Ravenna 7 (better cushioning, support, and flexibility); Hoka One One Vanquish (substantial midsole, maximum cushioning, and good support); and New Balance 860v8 stability running shoes (designed for runners who need support and delivers a stable ride for overpronators).

These were the shoe models that diligent salespeople at Dick's Sporting Goods and Georgetown Running Company told me through the years that I needed for my foot shape.

This time, I didn't listen. A few weeks before Ironman Lake Placid, I bought a pair of New Balance 1400v6 Revlites *online*. No fitting. No testing. No expert guidance. Why did I do this? Because at 7.2 ounces, they were much lighter than shoes I had worn in the past, which typically weighed from ten to twelve ounces. You may scoff at a difference of three ounces, but we serious Ironmen seek every advantage. If the loss of three ounces shaved a second off my race time, it was worth it!

The catch? These shoes had much less cushioning than my other shoes and lacked the arch support that my feet specifically needed.

I had read *Born to Run*, about the Tarahumara, a reclusive tribe of running legends who basically wear flip-flops with a thin rubber sole and can run forever, like Forrest Gump. I had gotten hooked on the minimalist shoe movement and spent many hours running on the balls of my feet in the style of a four-year-old. I had researched studies like the one conducted by the *Medicine & Science in Sports & Exercise* that stated that runners who wore shoes with features like added cushioning were likelier to get injured.

I had bought into all of it. But none of that was what made me switch. What made me switch is I wanted to be faster, and the featherweight 1400v6 Revlite racers made me feel fast. I was excited to share my latest discovery with Jim.

"Jim, I decided that I'm not going to use the shoes I've been wearing. I'm going to buy fresh ones for the Ironman and run in those."

"Here we go again," Jim said. "When will you learn?"

"You mock what you don't understand. I always get a fresh pair for the race. The only thing I'm worried about is I'm going with ones that don't have arch support. I've always worn shoes with lots of arch support because I have flat feet."

"You're an idiot. So tell me, what are you going with this time?"

"I'm going with New Balance 1400v6 Revlite racers. I just ordered them online."

"You ordered the shoes you're going to run an Ironman in online? You didn't want to test them first, make sure, oh, I don't know, that they fit?"

"It'll be fine. I'll test them out first, and if I hate them, I'll just wear the old ones."

"The race is in two weeks! You're really going to try to break in shoes in two weeks? You're supposed to be tapering."

"Stop being so dramatic!" I said. "I'll call you when I get them and let you know."

A few days later, my 1400v6 racers arrived in the mail. I tried them out for a three-mile run and LOVED them. I called Jim.

"Jim, I'm like Usain Bolt in these. I'm definitely wearing them for Placid."

"How far did you run?" he asked.

"Three miles."

"You really are a moron. You do realize that three miles is probably too small a sample size? Why don't you try them on a long run—oh, I forgot, you don't do any runs longer than six miles."

"Listen," I said. "All I know is that it's got 'Silent Hunter' written right on the inside sole. That's me, baby! Like a chee-tah stalking its prey. I'm going to be one fast mofo out there!"

"Do we have to go through this again?" Jim said. "You're more like a baby cheetah stalking a water buffalo, not realizing he's about to make a grave mistake. You should know by now to leave the silent hunting to the grown-ups and settle for the scraps."

Jim could talk reason to me all he wanted. This race, I wanted speed, so I was going to stick with the lighter, faster, arch-support-lacking silent hunter. It was not hard to predict how my knees were going to feel around mile 20.

TIP: Go to a serious, specialized running store and have someone test your running gait. A knowledgeable salesperson will evaluate your stride and find the correct shoe for you. I recommend a place like Potomac River Running in Washington, DC. They have you run on a treadmill and make a slow-motion video to examine your gait. Then they find you a shoe from their wide selection that complements it.

Mile 2 (116.4)
I emerged from town unscathed and now passed the same horse show grounds I had passed during the bike. The ski jumps loomed over the trees to the right. I spied a fat guy just ahead of me. Yes, you do encounter a few men and women I'd call fat, or at least large. Ironman calls them Clydesdales.

That is an actual designation. Many marathons have this designation too.

Jim, weighing in at anywhere from 214 to 225 pounds, is considered a Clydesdale. Imagine the blow to the confidence that that must strike. Here you are, running to lose weight. You're beginning to feel good about yourself. You get to the race and they say, "You're over here in the division named after a 2,000-pound horse." Was the fat hippo division already full?

The man was sweating and wheezing like those guys in the commercials with the elephant sitting on their chests. Disregarding all pacing plans and discipline and restraint, I sped up to pass him. I'd wreck my race, but I was damn sure I wasn't going to let a wheezing 250-pound guy with a beer gut run faster than me.

I passed him, smugly—so smugly. *Glad I'm not that guy!* Slightly edging a guy who weighed twice as much as me should have given no cause for cockiness. Perhaps the white-haired elderly gentleman who blew by me in the Half Ironman in Maryland earlier that summer thought something similar about me. *Poor bastard. He looks like hell and he's half my age! Glad I'm not that guy!* You'd think I'd have learned some humility then, but you'd be wrong. No matter, I'd learn it later.

Speaking of humility, as I ran, I saw a lot of calves ahead of me imprinted with a tattoo of the Ironman logo. It's basically a red letter "m" with a circle on top of it.

Jim got one on his left calf. I told him I liked it. "My calf or the tattoo?" he asked. He thinks he's Phil Mickelson now. It'll be thirty below in January, and he'll wear shorts to show off his calf muscles.

On one hand, I think the Ironman calf tattoo looks tacky and braggadocious. But on the other, I understand it and secretly want one myself. You destroyed your body and completed an epic, challenging race. You earned the right to let the world know you're a badass.

I let Karoline know she married a badass at least daily. "Do you know I'm an Ironman?" is my preferred response to any number of her concerns.

"It's too hot to run today," she might suggest.

"I don't know if you remember this, but I am an Ironman."

"There's thunder and lightning. I don't think you should bike in that."

"You do know that I am an Ironman, don't you?"

"Be careful, honey. That car engine is really heavy."

"Heavy for people who aren't an Ironman."

"It's probably not a good idea to eat that whole large pizza and tub of ice cream."

"Not a good idea if you're not an Ironman!"

Maybe I will get a tattoo someday to commemorate my Ironman status. Maybe when I know I'm strong enough to withstand the ridicule Karoline will heap upon me.

I slogged along, feeling out my muscles to see what they would give me. Journey's "Don't Stop Believin'" was blaring from speakers set up in the back of a spectator's pickup truck. Crowds along the route play music to try to get the runners going. Sometimes there are live bands. But the music from the crowd doesn't give me much of a boost. I need *my* playlist, playing loudly on earphones. That list includes a good sampling of Led Zeppelin and the Canadian pianist Glenn Gould. It's a very specific playlist.

Unfortunately, you're not allowed to wear headphones during the race. I wish I could. It's amazing how Bach's Keyboard Concerto in D Minor can take you to a place where you forget about sore legs. And it's so much easier to run through the pain cave with "Whole Lotta Love" blasting in your ears.

When I lived at the U.S. Embassy in Baghdad in 2009, I entered a 5K race—two loops around the embassy compound. Roughly sixty people ran that day. I put my headphones on and played the live, turbocharged version of Led Zeppelin's "Rock and Roll" from the *How the West Was Won* album on repeat for the entire race.

I shot out of the starting gate and continued sprinting right to the end, managing to hold first place most of the way, thanks mainly to Jimmy Page. Eventually an experienced marathoner and a Marine with quads the size of my waist caught up with me. I came in third, proud as a peacock.

Unfortunately, I paid the price for my exertion immediately, driven to my knees by a spasm of coughing. I continued hacking incessantly for three days. Turns out that sprinting in the sweet toxin-infused, burning-rubber-scented Iraqi air was not good for one's lungs. Not my first, and not my last, running mistake.

I continue to play music every time I run during training. And while I run, I thrash around like a spastic three-year-old, air drumming and singing, forgetting all about pace and pain. "What the hell are you doing?" Jim asked once when we did a long training run together.

"Getting the Led out."

"The only Led you need to get out is the lead in your ass."

~

I was out of town now, and the crowds were less dense but still scattered along the route, cheering loudly from their lawn chairs. I ran along Route 73, came to a steep downhill in front of the ski jumps, and turned left onto River Road.

Miles 3–9 (117.4–123.4)

The crowds are nonexistent on River Road. Nothing but you, other runners, fields, woods, and a massive red barn. The road is mostly flat, with a few rolling hills. It's the opposite vibe you get when running in town, which is noisy and boisterous. This part of the course is peaceful and serene, and you can get lost in your thoughts.

This is the gift running gives you. It's time and space to clear the head and think. When I'm on training runs, I seek out scenic routes. I want to be inspired. I want to get lost in my thoughts. I take time to think about things I want to do in life, like take a hot shower.

I think about how fortunate I've been, how blessed I've been to have my lovely little family and a wide circle of friends. I smell the crisp air and scent of wood-burning stoves in the fall and the sweetness of flowers in spring. I smell nothing in winter because it's too cold to run in winter. Overall, though, running is good for the soul.

Now I was reveling in the beauty of a late summer afternoon in the Adirondacks. There's nothing better. I felt good. Not James Brown shout-it-from-the-stage good. More Elvis in the late 1970s, sweating at the piano but still able to belt out "Unchained Melody"-good. I was in a nice, if slow, flow. The stomach issues were gone. The legs still had some juice. I hit the turnaround on River Road and started to head back toward the ski jumps.

I turned right onto Route 73 at the ski jumps and now had to run up the steep hill there. It's only about a hundred yards, but it feels like a mile. I walked up. Many people do. Spectators kept telling me to run. "Come on, Russell. Run up that hill! You can do it!" I wanted to punch them in the face. No, I can't.

Mile 10–11 (124.4–125.4)

Thanks to my decision to eschew arch support, my knees had succumbed to a steady soreness—a little pinch each time a foot hit the pavement. *You asshole*, I could hear them saying. *You just had to use shoes with no support. And we're the ones who end up paying for your stupidity.*

My modus operandi was to plod along with a steady stride and stop at each aid station, which were every mile. I never set a strict pace. I've always just gone by how my body feels and what it will give me. Someday I might push it harder and try to maintain an eight-minute per mile rumble and gallop by the aid stations. But not today.

Today, each aid station was like a beacon to a sailor lost at sea in a storm. Who am I kidding? For me, every Ironman marathon is really just a shuffle from one aid stop to the next. You've never seen someone get so excited about chicken broth in a Dixie cup, which was only served after dark. Other delicacies at Lake Placid's aid stations include Gatorade Endurance, water, bananas, pretzels, Coca-Cola, Red Bull, energy gels, fruit, and sundry performance bars.

This is not quite the spread of Marathon du Médoc, a marathon in the wine growing region of France that starts with a sip of wine, followed by a jaunt through vineyards where runners are treated to twenty-three wine tasting stops, fifty orchestras, twenty-one gourmet food stalls, oyster tasting and steak. This was the marathon I should have been running. Instead of marking my time with steak and Médoc, I was measuring my progress in gel packs.

As it was, after nine hours of sweet and sugary drinks, gels, and Honey Stinger Waffles, I was dying for something savory, and I looked forward to the broth more than I had ever looked forward to any filet in my life. Jim and I always had a loose goal to finish before dark, but that had never happened. While we were disappointed not to meet that aspiration, for me at least, chicken broth was a worthy consolation.

Perhaps the most critical items the aid stations offer are sponges soaked in ice. I pined for them almost as ardently as I did for broth. On a hot day, these sponges are better than a Swedish massage given by Ingrid Bergman while listening to ABBA. I luxuriated in them, squeezing the cold water onto my steaming head and stuffing them in my sweaty shirt.

TIP: Always take a couple of ice-water-soaked sponges if available. Stick them under the collar of your shirt at the back of your neck. If the sponges aren't available, take a cup of ice and pour it down your shirt. Always wear a hat or visor during the run so you can also keep ice and ice-water sponges on your head. This will keep you cool during hot weather.

I came to the aid station around mile ten and ate a third of a banana, drank some Gatorade, poured ice over my head, lingered a moment, and went on my way. The hills into town were coming up. The crowds cheered for me. "Russell, you're doing great. Just a few more miles, and you'll be an Ironman!" They thought I was on my second loop and almost done. I was not. I was still on the first loop. Did I look that wrecked?

Miles 12–13 (126.4–127.4)

I walked most of the way up the hills and finally made the turn onto Mirror Lake Drive, where the course turned from a slight incline to a slight decline. I came to Jim, Mark, and Jeff. They were at their tent at the side of Mirror Lake drinking beer and eating BBQ they had picked up from the Pickled Pig. I was almost at the end of my first loop. "How am I doing?" I yelled.

"You're as slow as shit coming out of a constipated old woman!" Jim yelled. "What happened to the silent hunter? You look more like a wildebeest on the wrong side of a lion attack!"

"If you're wondering how we're doing, we're surviving," Mark added as he took a drink of his Ubu Ale.

Nice friends I have.

ENDURANCE...OR WHEN IS THIS STUPID RACE GOING TO BE OVER?

Suffering is what I know how to do best.
— Jessie Diggins, cross country
skiing Olympic gold medalist

Ironman participants endure much during the race.

They suffer much during the training for the race.

Sometimes they persevere through at least four of the nine circles of Dante's hell just to register for a race and then actually get to it.

Until recently, after Ironman Mont Tremblant was added to the roster and the Canadians decided to stay on their side of the border, Ironman Lake Placid typically sold out within seconds. As I mentioned, my first encounter with this lunacy was when Jim and I both tried to sign up for the 2011 Ironman Lake Placid. We were both logged onto the website registration page and ready to register the second it opened. To increase our chances, we also had the registration phone number pre-dialed.

The moment the clock struck 10 a.m., I entered my credit card information and pounded the "register" button— BAM!—like I was a contestant on *Family Feud* and the question was "Name dumb shit husbands do that make their wives angry." I knew exactly what the survey would say for that one.

It turned out I was not on *Family Feud* but *Jeopardy!*, metaphorically matched up against Wild Bill Hickok of the clicker—trivia master and fast-twitch button pusher James Holzhauer. I had no chance. Seconds after I slammed the Enter key, my Ironman dream was dashed when a message popped up telling me the race was already sold out.

I frantically dialed the phone number. Busy signal. I tried for the next ten minutes. Busy signal.

"Hey, did you get in?" Jim asked.

"No, you?"

"I didn't even get the bra off."

Frustrated, we searched for a loophole. And found one: the volunteer hack.

After vigorous research, we learned that volunteers at an Ironman get priority to sign up for the following year's race. All they have to do is keep riders from crashing into pedestrians or hand out special needs bags for a couple of hours and then show up the next morning and wait in line to register during an hour-long window before they opened to the general populace.

We set our alarm for 3 a.m. and drove to the high school near the Olympic Oval. A line a quarter mile long had already formed by 4 a.m. We carried our sleeping bags and canvas chairs—the kind parents bring to soccer games to watch their kids—and set up camp at the back of the line for the long wait.

The doors didn't open until 9 a.m. The people closest to the front of the line had literally camped overnight. They had set up tents and slept there. At least a dozen tents dotted the length of the mass of bleary-eyed humans ahead of us.

"What if we got here too late?" I asked Jim. "What if we don't get to the front by the time they open to the general public and they tell us they already sold out? They don't guarantee volunteers a spot. They just give us the chance to register an hour before they open it up to the world."

"They'll guarantee us a spot, or I'll storm the gate and take a giant crap on their table." Jim said. "I didn't stand in the heat for four hours yesterday directing traffic or get up at 3 a.m. with your sorry ass to get denied. They don't want to poke the bear."

"It's freezing," I said, pulling my sleeping bag up over my chin. "I can't imagine jumping in a lake to swim when it's this cold."

I hate the cold. When I think about jumping into the chilly, shivery water at 7 a.m., I think of the last scenes of the movie *Titanic* when all of the former passengers are bobbing like blue popsicles in their frozen, watery grave. Okay, yes, I may be dramatic, but if you want to know what goes through my mind before getting in that water, it's that.

"You're like Cam when he was three years old and didn't want to eat his peas," Jim griped. "Quit your bitching."

I gave him the middle finger. "Fuck you."

"Instead of whining like a little baby," he said, "why don't you make yourself useful and go see if a coffee shop is open and get us some coffee?" So I walked down the hill, across the Olympic Oval to Stewart's convenience store and gas station. I was familiar with Stewart's only because Uncle Bob liked to get a vanilla soft serve ice cream there every year after finishing the race. I poured two large black coffees into Styrofoam cups and trudged back to the line.

I returned to a dick-measuring contest. A group of guys were talking to our line neighbors about past races and their expectations for next year. Bold boasts cut the foggy, frigid air:

"I finished Arizona last year in fourteen hours, but I was fighting an injury the entire race. I expect to finish Placid next year in about eleven hours."

"I'm going to crush the bike and the run. I just need to work on my swim, then I should be in the hunt for a Kona slot.

"I'm definitely gunning for top ten in my age bracket. I've seen last year's top ten times, and I know I can beat those."

"I'm going to finish the swim in under an hour. Take that to the bank, son! And then I should be able to knock out the bike in under six hours and the run in under four."

That last one was me. I'm an idiot. You get caught up in this and sometimes can't help but put your penis on the table too.

"I'm going to kick your ass next year, you little bitch."

That was Jim, talking to me.

We sweated it out for the next five hours until the doors opened, and the line began moving. We got in, made the cut, and waved around our golden ticket confirmation sheet.

Three years later, we were *so* much smarter. We found a way to beat the line.

We volunteered for the 2015 Ironman Lake Placid so we could do the same thing and get priority for the 2016 race. That year, the registration for volunteers was not at the high school, but in the Olympic Center, which is attached to the Herb Brooks Arena—the same Herb Brooks Arena that hosted the greatest sporting event in the history of Earth—the Miracle on Ice.

After watching the last runners stagger across the finish line before the midnight cutoff, Jim, our friend Mark, and I found ourselves in the Hunan Oshaka, a Chinese-Japanese casual dining restaurant that was still open and still serving food. We sat at the bar and ordered beers. All they had left was Dos Equis. We renamed the restaurant Chimex and knew we were about to start an annual post-race tradition to rival Bob and his Stewart's soft serve.

At 1:30 a.m., as Pancho Hu closed down our Chimex bar, and after multiple bottles of Dos Equis and at least 140 shots of sake, I, the most interesting man on my barstool, came up with an idea. "Hey, instead of getting up in a couple hours and waiting in line and sweating whether we'll get a spot in next year's race, why don't we just go over right now and sleep in line?"

And thus it was that, at 1:45 a.m., Jim, Mark, and I found ourselves with our sleeping bags and pillows lying on the cold concrete floor in a hallway outside of the famous hockey arena—which seemed so small and parochial to me for having hosted such an iconic, global event—looking up at photos and glass-enclosed old trophies from the 1932 and 1980 Winter Olympics.

There was only one person in front of us, and I wasn't certain if he was registering for the race or just a homeless person who found a good opportunity to sleep indoors. He never stirred the entire night.

I settled in underneath a life-sized photo of figure skating legend Sonja Henie, gold medalist and star of the 1932 games. My sleeping bag was itchy, and I couldn't get comfortable.

"Hey Russ, are you getting aroused by Sonja or something? Are you rubbing one out or is there a squirrel running around in your sleeping bag?" Jim said. "What the hell is going on over there?"

"This sleeping bag is making me itch...and I'm trying to stay upwind of the toxic gases coming from the direction of your ass. She is nice though," I said, as Sonja, queen of the ice for a decade, loomed over me. "Hey, did a bear eat Mark and get in his sleeping bag or is that him snoring? How is he asleep already?"

On it went. We brave morons endured a night of loud snoring, Jim's Dos Equis-crab rangoon-infused farts, an itchy sleeping bag, and little sleep so we could be first in line to register for an event in which we would torture ourselves for 13-plus hours, swimming, running, and biking until our nipples bled and our toenails fell off.

Four months later, the race had not sold out. "Jim, I just checked and it's still open."

"You're telling me we slept all night on the fucking floor of a hockey rink to be first in line, and four months later, you can still register?"

"I'm afraid so." Stay stupid, my friends.

I digress. I was talking about endurance, and somehow, I stumbled down a rabbit hole on registration.

To get back on track...an Ironman athlete endures many things, but mainly the requirement to get up at 4 a.m. to swim, bike, and run more miles than a trip to the moon for a period of time ranging anywhere from six months to over a year.

You must persevere. Your body must withstand the almost comical trials you put it through: stress fractures, screaming muscles, sleep deprivation, and frostbite or heat stroke, depending on the season. If your body were your spouse, it would call the police on you to report domestic abuse.

That's all fine and dandy and par for the course. But that's the bunny slope of endurance. The real endurance—Wagner-Ring-Cycle endurance—is your family's ability to endure the crap you put them through during that same period.

"Honey, would you like to join me for a glass of wine?" your wife says seductively, wearing the Victoria's Secret negligee you got her at Christmas on the premise that it was a present for her and which she swore she would wear as soon as the first Mars colony was established. She is making a Herculean effort to show her love by wearing the least-favorite gift she's received *that* Christmas.

"No, sorry, sweetie," you say, glancing up briefly from *Triathlete Magazine*'s "best bikes to purchase now so you can make your friends jealous and qualify for Kona" issue. "I'm in training, and a spoonful of Nyquil is as close as I'm going to get to alcohol.

"Would it help if I wore spandex bike pants and athletic tape? she says as she storms off. You don't notice as you're too busy looking at elevation maps of the course.

"Daddy, I made you brownies. Will you try one?" your sweet four-year-old says.

"You spiteful child! Get that poison away from me!" you scream. "Why is everybody trying to tempt me??? Don't you know I'm in training and I will not put anything other than protein powder and chia seeds in my body? Jesus, sometimes I feel like a Vicodin abuser surrounded by meth addicts pushing me to join them in destroying my body!"

Let me count the many ways in which a family endures your wretchedness during Ironman training. That quality time your wife has planned for after the kids are in bed? Because you arise at 4 a.m. each day to stretch and go for a warm-up run of ten miles, you can't keep your eyes open beyond 8 p.m. Your head is already bobbing by dinnertime. No way you are going to make it through a movie.

She wants to have a conversation about life or about how the two-year-old called his daycare provider a jerk and has been walking around the house saying "Jesus Cripe" (just like Daddy). She wants to tell you about that guy on her team at work who is suing the company because he can't bring his cat to work as an emotional support animal.

Good luck with that. You'll be yawning the whole way through that drive across her feelings, a zombie from *The Walking Dead*, stumbling around with glazed eyes and drool rolling down your chin…and she'll be stewing, waiting for the day this stupid, stupid race is over and you return to the world of the living.

The worst of all offenses—and not because it is the hardest for your spouse to endure, but because it is the most antithetical to your priorities before signing up for an Ironman—is when she would like some sexy time and you turn into something unrecognizable from a male human being and tell her that you're too tired. "Can you just rub my temples while you watch *The Marvelous Mrs. Maisel* and I fall asleep with my head on your lap?"

Your wife endures your Ironman midlife crisis. And when she scolds you mildly for taking so much time away from her and the family and for spending money like a four-year-old let loose with a credit card in Toys "R" Us, how do you answer?

You say, "I may be having a midlife crisis, but at least I'm not snorting my money, gambling our house away, or banging my intern and buying her diamond earrings. I'm just running around in spandex."

She loves this answer.

CHAPTER 18
ARMS RACE

They're all bringing automatic weapons, and you're bringing a pea shooter.

— Jim Kane

If I wasn't gambling all my money away, where was it going? What exactly was I spending it on?

The first cost associated with Ironman is the registration fee to sign up for a race. It is the definition of lunacy to spend $750 for a day of torture, but we freely and gladly do it. And then we do it again…and again…and again. My mother always said it stops hurting when you stop banging your head against the wall. I must like the pain. The truth is that Ironman is a vortex that sucks you in. It's a banana peel you keep slipping on. It's an addiction equal in power to Trump's need to send nonsensical tweets at all hours.

I suppose you could do an Ironman on the cheap, with the registration fee representing your largest expense (still a sizeable amount). You could find a race near you and drive. You could find a local campsite and pitch a tent. You could borrow a bike or use your clanking Scattante. You could don your child's bike helmet and wear an old college tee shirt, a pair of shorts, and the sneakers you got for Christmas two years ago.

You could do all that. But that's not how it works. People actually want to finish the race and do well. And, let's be honest, you want to beat your friends and family for bragging rights. Cheap, crappy gear won't allow you to crow at Chimex for years after. Fishing tales have nothing on Ironman storytelling.

So when your friend Jim Kane issues a few warning shots by buying new Zipp wheels and hiring a run coach, you need to respond in kind.

When your other friend Steve Desio mounts a shock-and-awe campaign by putting a tri coach on retainer, building a custom-made Parlee TTir Tribike, and buying $1,200 Wahoo KICKR Power Trainer, you need to buy a few more bottles of oxygen water to try to stay in the conversation.

That's how it goes in the world of Ironman. You become Quint and Hooper on the Orca in Jaws one-upping each other's scars. They keep ramping up, raising the stakes, until Quint takes it to a level beyond reach with the *USS Indianapolis* speech:

One thing about an Ironman who doesn't buy a serviceable bike: he has lifeless legs, like a doll's legs…eleven hundred athletes went into the water…316 made it to the finish; the cheap sneakers, ill-fitting bikes and shoddy wetsuits took the rest.

Somehow, I'm always Chief Brody, just sitting on the sideline with nothing to show.

"Hey, Stevie D spent $400 on his helmet, and you're still wearing your $40 child's helmet from Target," Jim said. "Why don't you just cut out a giant Wiffle ball and put it on your head? You need to get with the program!"

"You guys are going to put me in the poor house if you keep spending money on run coaches and swim coaches and fancy wheels and helmets," I said. "I'm going to need to start a Kickstarter campaign to fund this thing."

To give you a sense of the spending, here are two comprehensive breakdowns of typical costs to do an Ironman. First, the "moderately priced" Ironman experience (mine):

- Registration: $685–$795, depending on which tier you get in

- Aero wheels, a direct-from-China brand ("Superteam"): $400

- House in Lake Placid: $5,100

- Flight: $350–$600

- Cost to ship bike: $300

- Bike fit: $395

- Velolabs twelve-week winter session: $300

- Nutritionist: $700

- Cervelo P2 Tri Bike: $1,959

- Tri Kit – Pro LTD Bib Short: $180

- Bike shirt – Sportful Bodyfit Pro Race Jersey: $120.

- Bike helmet - Kask Mojito16: $200

- Xterra Vortex 4: $400 (with Disney Tri Team discount)

- Training race (Eagleman 70.3): $325 for the registration fee and $373.42 for a one-night stay at Hyatt Regency

- Shroom tech ($63.49 x 2): $126.98

- Gels: $100

- Chiropractor/massage ($85 per session x five sessions): $420

- Running shoes: $160

- Cost of flight to volunteer the year before and ensure entry to next year: $350–$600

- LA Fitness membership and personal trainer ($29.95 x 12 months): $359.40

- Total: $13,412

- I forgot one. Add this to the tab:

- Two Kennedy Center box-seat tickets to Hamilton to ease my guilt: $1,425.

Here is a more upscale "all-in" Ironman experience (courtesy of my friend Steve Desio):

- House rental: $4,825

- Groceries: $300

- New Parlee TTir Tribike with custom paint and components: $11,386 (includes Zipp 404 wheelset: $850, Zipp 808 wheelset: $1,000)

- Swimming gear (bag, fins, paddles): $40

- Massages, once per month ($65 x 4 months): $260

- Gatorade Endurance ($28/jug x 6): $168

- GU gels ($51/case x 4): $204

- Vector 3 power meter pedals: $600

- Garmin Fenix 5 watch: $750

- Roka Wetsuit: $925

- Tri Coach ($370/month): $2,220

- Wahoo Kickr Power Meter: $1,200

- Bike Tires Continental Grand Prix 4000 S II: $160

- Zwift membership ($15/month): $180

- Scicon Bike travel case: $999

- Tri Shoes: $160

- Tri Suit: $160

- Bike Helmet: $200

- XLAB bike hydration system: $150

- Ironman merch tent: $500

- 70.3 warm-up race, registration fee: $300

Total: $25,687

Bar bill at Chimex after the race: PRICELESS!!

It costs Steve more money to do an Ironman than some people's annual incomes.

I may have hinted at a way to do an Ironman on the cheap, but that's about as realistic as trying to do a discounted week at Disney World. There is no "Ironman-on-the-cheap" version. That's just a fairytale.

Granted, some of the costs are accumulative, meaning you're not buying a bike every year (though you will likely upgrade once or twice). But many are recurring, meaning you will spend the dough every single time you do an Ironman.

My only successful attempt to save money was buying aero wheels direct from China. So instead of $4,000 reputable, proven Zipp wheels, I spent $400 on wheels that would be shipped to me from some guy's garage in Beijing.

"Jim, I ordered these tires that will ship direct from China. Some brand called Superteam. I think I got the right ones, but I'm not sure because most of the descriptions are in Mandarin. But they were only $400, so I'm saving a ton of money."

"Did you account for your hospital bills when your China-direct comes apart going down the Keene hill? You should add that to the costs."

TIP: Ironman has set up a tiered registration, meaning they have windows in which to register at a certain price before they increase prices. This is a recent development. They break them into four tiers: $685, $705, $750, and $795. Pricing is inventory-based according to slot quantities and will automatically increase when capacity has been filled. The sooner you can register, the more money you'll save. Figure out which race you want to do and sign up before they increase the costs. You can save up to $100.

It was bad enough to hemorrhage cash for products I'd use, services I needed, and races I'd run. But then I started just throwing money away. I might as well have just gone to the dog track or the bar and pissed it against the wall.

It started with Maryland Ironman in 2013. The draw? It was flat and fast and took place on the scenic Eastern Shore of Maryland—cattails and salt marshes, refuges and pristine creeks, ocean breezes and historic homes.

This was also when it was the ChesapeakeMan Ultra, before the World Triathlon Corporation bought it, branded it an "Ironman" race, and jacked up the cost. The ChesapeakeMan cost $435. Cheaper, but not cheap. Jim, big surprise, talked me into doing it.

I lived in California at the time, and Peter was four months old. First, where was my brain? Leaving Karoline with an infant so I could fly across the country was my first mistake.

The second was not packing my bike ahead of time. For those not aware, you cannot take a bike on an airplane unless it is packed in a box or a shipping case. I learned this the hard way when I tried to bring my bike with me on the plane to California and the ticket desk lady looked at me like I had three heads. Karoline had to take the bike back to the car, and I trained for my first Ironman on my friend's kid's rusted Huffy.

This time I at least got a bike case, which I borrowed from a Disney Tri Team member, and brought it to work. This was the third mistake: working the day I was flying. Work got busy, and I couldn't leave early.

When you pack a bike, you have to take off the pedals—at least the pedals—and often the handlebars as well. I couldn't get the pedals off. I had the tool, but the pedals were on extremely tight. As the clock ticked and the chances of me making my flight diminished, I called Jim.

"You moron!" he barked. "You're just packing your bike now? I don't understand how your brain works."

This was me. Jim would have had the bike packed a week ahead of time. He would not have left anything to the last minute. I told him I would find another flight leaving the next day. I looked, but the cheapest flight I could find was $800. I had already spent $333 on the flight I missed. I couldn't afford to spend $800 more.

I looked to see if there were any bargains on Saturday.

It wasn't ideal to fly across the country the day before a race. You're supposed to be checked in by Friday and have your bike racked on Saturday. It didn't matter. There was nothing. After an hour on Kayak trying to find a reasonable rate, I finally called it, like a surgeon calling a death.

Time: 5:20 p.m.

Date: Thursday before the Ironman.

Cause of Death: Stupidity.

Between registration and the cost of the flight, I had spent $768 for...nothing. I would have been down $200 more for the hotel, but Jim's tri coach took my place in the room and picked up my slack. At least if I'd lost the money while gambling, I'd have gotten a few drinks and a good steak in the bargain.

Then there was Chattanooga. Jim and Mark had talked me into signing up for the Chattanooga Ironman even though I was doing a half and a full Ironman already that year. Karoline was thrilled.

Actually, Karoline didn't know I was doing the race. I hope none of you will ever be as stupid as I am. I told her I was just going to Tennessee to support Jim, Mark, and Jeff, as they had supported me in Lake Placid earlier that summer. I was going there strictly for Sherpa duty.

In fairness, that was my original intent. I wasn't planning to do the race. But, as I've said, Ironman is a vortex. It sucks you in. My friends know my weaknesses, and they exploited them.

"You're already trained," Jim said. "You just have to show up and go. Lake Placid is a much harder course. You'll crush Chattanooga."

"Karoline will kill me," I offered.

"Probably. But listen, kid, it's all in how you present it," Jim said. "You've got to sell it. You're already going to be there. She cleared that."

"Okay. You've talked me into it. I'm signing up."

"The Russ Newell redemption tour starts in Chattanooga," Jim yelled into the phone. "Get on board the Choo Choo train!"

I signed up. But I didn't tell Karoline. In my defense, I didn't tell her because she is a worrier, and as soon as I told her, she'd be anxious all weekend. She'd worry that I'd drown in the swim. She'd worry that I'd crash on the bike. She'd worry that I'd have heat stroke on the run. I wanted to spare her from all this.

Let me save you the suspense. She found out. No dummy, she started to get suspicious when I continued to request to go on five-hour bike rides during the weekend and get up at 5 a.m. to get in a swim before work. "I thought your race was over," she said.

She went on the Ironman app to plug in Jim and Mark and Jeff so she could follow them. Then, on what must have been a complete lark, she typed in my name. Low and behold, I was a participant! This was not a happy night for me. After warning me to NEVER, EVER lie to her again—and no, protecting her from worry was not a good reason—she actually, impossibly said I could still do it.

On the Thursday before Sunday's race, I began the nine-hour drive from Reston, Virginia, to Chattanooga, Tennessee. An hour into the drive, Jim called. He and Mark and Jeff had arrived in Chattanooga the day before. "They've canceled the swim," he said.

"What? Why?"

"With all the rain, the river is swollen, and the current is too strong. They're saying it's unsafe."

"You've got to be kidding me. That sucks. I really want to do the swim. I trained for all three, and I want to do all three."

The thought of driving another eight hours and not getting to do all three disciplines didn't appeal to me. Based on my description of my Lake Placid swim, one might think I'd be thrilled to be able to skip the swim and go right to the bike. But it'd be like getting an incomplete grade. Nobody wants an incomplete—you want to finish and get an A. Or at least a B. Maybe B-. But still better than INCOMPLETE followed by summer school.

As with reading achievement tests, you want to measure progress. Weird, I know. You want to know if you trained well enough to get a PR. I think that is always one motivation for continuing to do this insane race—you learn something every time you do one, and you find little things you can improve upon. *If I just timed that gel better, I wouldn't have run out of gas at mile 75. If I had taken enough salt, I wouldn't have cramped. If I didn't take a pepper shot, I wouldn't have shit myself all day.*

If I couldn't measure myself with an entire race, I'd rather turn around, save some chits with Karoline, and find a race to do the following year. Then Jim gave me an idea. An awful idea. A wonderful, awful idea.

"You do know that Maryland is also on Sunday," he said, referring to Ironman Maryland held on the same exact course where I had done the 70.3 race just a couple months ago. "And you know Diane and Mary are doing it. She rented a house. I'm sure they'd let you stay with them."

"Is it still open?"

"I don't know. Call Diane. She'll be able to find out."

I called Diane, who had been Jim, Mark, and Jeff's coach. She happened to be at the Ironman Village checking in. "Hey Diane, the Chattanooga swim is canceled, and I'm thinking about turning around and driving to Maryland instead. Can you find out if it's open and if I can transfer my registration to Maryland?"

She found a race official and confirmed that I could register for Maryland, but I'd have to pay. "Seriously?" I said. "I paid for a full race in Chattanooga and I'm not getting a full race through no fault of my own, and they're going to make me pay again to do Maryland?"

Diane asked again. "Yes, you have to pay."

I weighed it:

Continue to Chattanooga, $750 fee already paid, be away from home Thursday through Monday.

Turn around and go home, satisfied that I'd already done two Ironman races that year.

Pay another $750 (I love spending money!!!), turn around, cut my drive by six hours, do a full Ironman, with swim, and only be away from home Friday through Sunday.

This time I called Karoline to run it by her. It was a better deal for her because I'd be away two less nights. That meant two more nights at home, assisting with the bedtime routine, helping when all three kids woke up in the middle of the night like little vampires sucking our sanity.

She gave me the green light, and I turned the car around, vowing to find some race director that would let me transfer my Chattanooga race fee to Maryland. I never found one. Everyone I spoke to told me that even though the Chattanooga swim had been canceled, they do not allow you to transfer fees. So it was going to be, at minimum, a $1,500 weekend. At least Diane and her friend Mary let me sleep on their couch and I didn't have to pay another $1,000 for a hotel room.

Unfortunately, Chattanooga wasn't the last time I blew a bunch of money on a race I never ran. In December 2018, I tried to register for the Half Ironman in Williamsburg, Virginia. It was sold out.

Lucky for me, Ironman has a foundation that sets aside a percentage of your fee to go towards grant funding and service project opportunities in partnership with local nonprofit organizations that benefit the community where the race is being held. If a race has sold out, there are almost always some slots available if you're willing to pay a little extra.

I did this for Williamsburg, buying a $600 Ironman Foundation Community Fund entry—double the regular entrance fee—to support athletic, education, health, human services, and public benefit organizations in a community I had never set foot in. And then I skipped the race. I love giving money away!

Why did I skip? The Ironman was in May. The winter and spring were cold. I hadn't trained, so I wasn't ready. Damn you, Jim, why do you have to always be right! I also didn't want to repeat Maryland 70.3 and leave Karoline to schlep the kids around Colonial Williamsburg by herself while I endured pain, trauma, possible danger, and more guilt.

I sent a series of emails to Williamsburg Ironman a week before the race begging them to transfer my Williamsburg fee to the Lake Placid 70.3, which was in the fall, and for which I might have found more time to train during the warm days of summer. The silence I heard from them let me know I'd never see that money again.

All was not lost, however. A few days after the race I received a nice email from Ironman Foundation:

General entry athletes cross the finish line and that's it. For IRONMAN Foundation Athletes, race day may be over, but your legacy remains. Your impact will carry on and continue to create positive, tangible change in Williamsburg and in its surrounding communities, long after race day.

When I couldn't afford to take Karoline to a nice dinner for our anniversary, it would sure soothe her to know that my legacy in Williamsburg was secure. *Honey, McDonald's value meals will have to do this year. I'm creating positive change for the people of Williamsburg.* She'd understand.

Oh, and for my generosity, I also received in the mail a beautiful water bottle with Ironman Foundation written on it. A gorgeous $600 water bottle.

Then I got a follow-up glowing tribute from Ironman to make me feel good about myself:

> *Thank you for your support and dedication. Athletes like you truly embody our mantra of "Service Through Sport, Commitment to Community."*

I sure did. What a peach. My wife would be so proud. At least in the divorce she couldn't take all our money and possessions, because we'd have none. Unless she wanted a $200 bike helmet.

CHAPTER 19

DO IT FOR THE KIDS

I'm bad, and that's good. I will never
be good, and that's not bad.
— Bad Guy Affirmation, *Wreck-It Ralph*

My spending was out of control, so I began to seek ways to cut costs.

One tactic I tried to deploy to take away the sting of guilt and make me feel less selfish was to sign on with a team raising money for a worthy cause. You name the cause, and there are people running on behalf of it. Swim to save the dolphins! Bike to combat climate change! Run for Roseanne Barr!

Many causes raise money to find cures for horrible diseases like cancer, ALS, or cystic fibrosis. Some focus on raising funds for those who are sick or injured and can't afford to pay hospital bills. Others help communities or build facilities like running tracks or playgrounds.

In 2017, I found one that allowed me to waive the registration fee in exchange for raising money and awareness—the Multiple Myeloma Research Foundation, which was the official charity partner of 2017 Ironman Lake Placid.

Multiple myeloma is a rare, incurable blood cancer related to lymphoma and leukemia. After suffering through symptoms like anemia, renal impairment, bone weakness, infections, nausea, and vomiting, about 12,000 people die each year from the disease.

So instead of paying a $750 Ironman Lake Placid 2017 entry fee, I signed up with MMRF's Team for Cures and committed to raising $5,000 for cancer research. I had to give my credit card information as insurance, the idea being that if I didn't raise the money, they would deduct it from my card.

After I signed on, I got an email message from Kelley Ward, my MMRF team leader:

> *Thank you for joining MMRF Team for Cures!*
> *Your participation and fundraising bring hope*
> *and much needed attention to so many with this*
> *fatal disease. Together we can help extend the*
> *lives of loved ones everywhere.*

It was going to be so great to do an Ironman with this team and raise money for a good cause. To bring hope! To extend lives!

MMRF would set me up with my own fundraising page that I could personalize. I scanned a few of my new teammates' fundraising pages to get ideas about what to say in mine.

The MMRF is one of the most highly regarded cancer foundations in the world. Nearly 90% of the total MMRF budget goes directly towards research and related programming. The MMRF is in the top 1% of all charities, having earned Charity Navigator's 4-star rating for 16 years...

And now the MMRF is funding 20 additional treatments in various stages of development, giving hope to tens of thousands of patients and families like ours...

Thanks to the important work of the MMRF and our partners, the FDA has approved ELEVEN new treatments in the time that it usually takes for ONE new drug to come to market. There are more treatment options in the pipeline...

Training for this event is a big challenge, but nothing compared to the challenges faced by patients with multiple myeloma.[1]

That was good. I'd use it. Then I'd take it next-level and start a blog to share the stories and struggles of the amazing

---

1 Gavin Pritchard, "Welcome to My IRONMAN Fundraising Page," Multiple Myeloma Research Foundation, July 28, 2019, https://endurance.themmrf.org/2019IMLP/Tri4Cancer.

people—particularly kids if I could find them—for whom I was sacrificing my body and serenity:

> *Meet little Bobby Belzak. He has bone marrow transplant surgery next week, but he tells his mommy he'll be brave like his hero Spiderman. Look at seven-year-old Suzy Steele. She has radiation each day where doctors inject poison into her emaciated thirty-five-pound body, but she still greets everyone with a smile. Little Johnny Goodwin's kidneys are failing, and he needs to be hooked up to a machine to live, but he finds a way each day to go for a walk outside in the hospital courtyard and feed the birds.*

That's nice, but can little Bobby and Johnny swim, bike, and run 140.6 miles in thirteen hours? No. So I'm sacrificing my own comfort to do it for them.

Karoline will be so moved by how I am inspiring sick youngsters and bringing hope to countless others by raising money for them—and not spending our own meagre funds—that she'll light up with joy the next time I say I'm doing an Ironman.

I'll run with pictures of the kids I'm sponsoring printed on my shirt. I'll write their names on my sneakers. Their parents, with whom I'll become close friends, will download the Ironman tracker and monitor my progress. Fans cheering along the course will yell, "You're amazing, Russell! So selfless! You can do it!!"

When I finish the race, local news will interview me. "How does it feel to be a hero? How does it feel to inspire so many people?"

"Well Judy, the kids are the real heroes. What I just endured is no doubt incredible, but it's nothing compared to the suffering these kids with multiple myeloma experience every day."

Thank Christ my credit card was compromised a few months later, because I only raised $100, which was my own donation to prime the tip jar. I was on the hook for $4,900, which the Multiple Myeloma Research Foundation would have deducted if some gas station rat didn't steal my info, prompting the credit card company to issue me a new card with a new number.

"Wow. You're a dirtbag. I can't believe you're stiffing a cancer charity," Jim said.

"I meant well," I said. "I really did. I don't know why I thought I could train for an Ironman and raise money for a charity with a newborn and two honey badgers tearing up the house…. Do you think they'll track me down and figure out a way to deduct the $5,000 from my account?"

"I hope so."

"Some friend you are. You're supposed to make me feel better. Don't forget we were in the middle of a move to a new house too. It was a perfect storm."

"You're full of excuses," Jim said. "I'm going to start calling you Britney Spears. "Oops!...I Did It Again." When will you learn?"

Nora had arrived in January, joining a four-year-old and a two-year-old to suck up every spare second of time Karoline and I had. In April, we began moving from our 980 square foot condo in Washington, DC, to a house in the suburbs. Had I taken the time to do one or the other—fundraise or train—I would have pushed the limits of Karoline's indulgence of my ill-conceived hobby and found myself moving back to that 980 square foot condo by myself.

So I was not going to be a hero, a slayer of cancer. More... slug. Jim and Mark were appalled and entertained by my dilemma. "They are going to track you down," Jim said daily. "They'll find a way to get their money. In fact, I might call and help them."

When Jim and I arrived at Lake Placid in 2017 to support Mark's wife, Kara, who was running her first Ironman, I was still listed as a participant in the race. "You'll be doing dishes at the Multiple Myeloma Research Foundation Team pancake breakfast tomorrow," Mark added helpfully.

I skulked around Lake Placid all weekend and looked woefully at those saviors of children bonding in fellowship and rejoicing in their goodness at the Multiple Myeloma tent. I vowed that someday I'd redeem myself and help them. Since one of MMRF's goals is to spread awareness, here, at least, is a small thing I can do—share the MMRF Success Story:[2]

- The mission of the MMRF is to relentlessly pursue innovative means that accelerate the development of next-generation multiple myeloma treatments to extend the lives of patients and lead to a cure.

- Since its inception in 1998, the MMRF has raised more than $250 million, making it the world's leading private funder of myeloma research.

- The work of the MMRF contributed to the FDA approval of six drugs for multiple myeloma in just eleven years—a track record unparalleled in oncology.

- Nearly 90 percent of the MMRF budget is directed to myeloma research and related programs.

———

Sadly, MMRF wasn't the only bird-brained idea I had to save money and help others in need that went awry. One evening, I was invited to a presentation at a prestigious French restaurant in Great Falls, Virginia, where a woman named Caroline Gaynor talked about guiding blind athletes in Ironman competition.

———

2   "About the MMRF," Multiple Myeloma Research Foundation, https://themmrf. org/about/.

It was a presentation she gave for her company, Dimensional Fund Advisors, wherein she compared a blind athlete's need to have someone guide them through the Ironman to that of a novice investor needing an expert to guide them through the thickets of the financial world.

Somewhere during the presentation, I learned that the blind athlete paid the registration fee.

Are you kidding me? This is a thing? Someone else pays the $750 for you to swim and run with them tethered to you? And you ride a tandem bike, so there are two people peddling?

After she finished her presentation, I walked up and introduced myself as a fellow Ironman and thanked her for enlightening me on blind athlete guiding and investing. I began peppering her with questions. Perchance thinking I was hitting on her and not just overly eager to share my Ironman bona fides and validate that I would be a good guide, she reenacted McKayla Maroney receiving silver in the vault and packed up her stuff to leave.

After some deliberation, perhaps not enough, I sent her an email the following week.

Caroline - I heard you speak at the L'Auberge Chez Francois and I'm fascinated by the idea of helping guide a blind athlete. I'm interested in doing it and I'd love to talk to you about it sometime. How do you get involved?

She did not reply. I sent a few follow-up emails. She did not respond. Maybe she feared that I was going to cut into her business, steal some of her clients. I mean, there couldn't be that many visually impaired triathletes in need of someone to guide them through an Ironman, could there?

I sought answers elsewhere and contacted Athlete Services at the World Triathlon Corporation. A nice lady named Michelle told me about an organization called United in Stride that helps unite visually impaired runners and sighted guides.

I entered my name into their database, eager to find an impaired runner to help. A woman named Gwendolyn sent me a message about her twelve-year-old son, Daniel. He had grown frustrated by his loss of vision and wanted to run in some upcoming races.

I responded and said I'd be happy to help train with young Daniel.

She wrote back telling me that Daniel was super excited to run with me. She sent me a schedule of races that spring that he wanted to run in—two 5Ks and a youth triathlon.

I told her that sounded good to me. I didn't hear back from her, and a year passed with no blind athlete ever contacting me to ask for my assistance. Then, out of the blue, the mom sent me an email apologizing for the delay in responding.

She said that Daniel had had an injury, and then a busy summer, and then Boy Scouts, and then the weather was so bad during the winter, yada, yada, yada. She said he still

wanted to run in some races and asked if I was available evenings and weekends to train with him.

I thought about this. On one hand, it would be extremely
rewarding to help this boy. I pictured picking him up.
Gwendolyn would greet me in the driveway with coffee and
blueberry muffins. Daniel and I would wave goodbye as she
beamed in the driveway. I'd feel good. Hero status restored.

But then different thoughts came to me. First, it was weird
that she went dark for a year and then reached out again so
suddenly. Second, I didn't feel vetted enough. Didn't she want
to interview me first? Conduct an FBI investigation? How did
she know I wasn't some pedophile creeper preying on young
blind kids?

Would Chris Hansen greet me when I arrived at the
house? "Why don't you take a seat, Russell." he'd say, pulling
up a kitchen barstool. "You say you just wanted to run, and
yet you have Vaseline and a six pack of Gatorade in the car.
Explain yourself."

"Goddammit Chris, the Vaseline is for my nipples and
undercarriage so they don't chafe when I run!! I swear!!"

I had another hesitation. I had three kids of my own. With
a hectic work and training schedule, time with them was precious. I couldn't justify spending weekend hours with someone else's kid when I had my own that needed their dad to play
hide and seek, build Lego sets, and make blueberry pancake

breakfasts. Where was Daniel's fucking dad? Maybe he should get his ass off the couch and go running with little Danny.

Screw it, I decided. I didn't want to be on the lam from a cancer charity or end up on *To Catch A Predator*. I'd suck it up and just spend the money.

I paid full freight for my 2018 Lake Placid Ironman slot and then drove to the liquor store to buy five Powerball and five Mega Millions tickets.

CHAPTER 20

CARNAGE—
SECOND LOOP RUN

An Ironman IS never fun…an Ironman WAS fun.
— Jim Kane

Mile 13 (127.4)

Down the steep hills through town again. It was sunny and hot at this point. I was hot and not so sunny. A few people in this section of the race, God bless them, put out sprinklers or stood with a hose and sprayed willing passing runners. I was more than willing—I sought them out.

I also sought out the BASE Salt salespeople who always set up a tent in the same spot just outside of town. Each year, they eagerly hand out plastic vials of what they call their electrolyte salt.

> *BASE Electrolyte Salt provides athletes with superior electrolyte replenishment, enabling them to maximize performance, stay hydrated, and fight fatigue,* announces the website. *More than just*

> *sodium chloride, BASE Salt's all-natural formula*
> *contains 84 essential minerals needed to main-*
> *tain proper energy and fluid balance and avoid*
> *muscle cramps.*

BASE also claims to prevent gastrointestinal distress, which was an Imodium wet dream to my churning stomach. They often run out toward the end of the race, so I grabbed three vials. I poured one down my greedy little throat and stashed the others in the back pocket of my shirt.

I had taken BASE salt every race and had never cramped up during the run or had any distress with my muscles, so I trusted them.

Mile 14 (128.4)
Just beyond the BASE people, I came upon a group of guys, who were dressed in thongs and handing out cold beers. While enticing, I declined. I did not trust them.

I was surprised that any athlete took these thonged gentlemen up on their offer, but a few did. I wondered where else in life would you ingest something given to you on the street by a complete stranger wearing a thong? Maybe outside a crack house. But is that really the model you want to follow? Yet here I was, appreciatively taking vials of pink salt from a cheerful stranger. *Hey, you got any pepper shots too?*

Mile 15 (129.4)

I passed the airport and headed down the hill by the ski jump. Athletes running (or walking or sitting on the curb) opposite me up the hill looked defeated. I turned onto River Road, the long, meandering road outside of town where most of the run took place, and settled in.

TIP: Walk the aid stations. It's better to be humble and walk before you have to.

Mile 16 (130.4)

I ran down River Road alongside a rugged split rail fence encircling a serene field. The road was flat. I passed the massive red barn. This, to me, is the prettiest part of the course.

As I've said, running can be good for the soul, with exercise firing up those charming endorphins that make you feel good after a training run—well, after a training run, a shower, and a nap. All sorts of benefits are derived from running. For example, an *International Journal of Workplace Health Management* study concluded that running and preparing for a marathon improves job performance, boosts productivity, and increases creativity.

The same study said because preparing for a marathon requires planning, discipline, dedication, and perseverance, it also leads to a significant improvement in your overall personality and character.[1]

"Yeah, that study is garbage," Karoline said when I told her about it. "My unofficial research has concluded that you become a selfish, cranky pain in the ass, and your productivity at home is nonexistent when you're training."

As far as improving job performance, I don't know how productive I am when I'm falling asleep at my desk in the afternoon staff meetings because I got up at 4 a.m. that morning to run ten miles.

I was slowing down at this point, earning a PhD in the Ironman shuffle. Just keep moving the feet, survive and advance, I told myself over and over. But I was not in too much pain, and I was enjoying the serenity of the pastoral surroundings. That would end soon.

Mile 17 (131.4)

You measure your marathon progress mile marker by mile marker. I was now just trying to make it to the next marker. Each subsequent one seemed farther and farther away and more difficult to reach. And each time I made one, I felt an enormous sense of accomplishment and relief. Only nine more to go.

---

1   Sadi Kahn, "74 Benefits of Running Backed by Science," RunRepeat, August 27, 2020, https://runrepeat.com/what-running-does-to-your-body.

Mile 18 (132.4)

I was beginning to move like Frankenstein's monster, including the loud groaning and the self-loathing. I had to take a crap in the porta potty—hopefully the last—but I couldn't crouch down low enough. I braced myself on the toilet roll dispenser, using it to support my weight so I could get low enough to make sure everything got into the bowl.

As my face set into a grimace befitting the grind of the run, I recalled watching just two days ago roughly twenty-five runners sashay down Main Street in their underwear. Laughing. Having fun. They were part of a group that jogs one and a half miles in their skivvies each year in something called the Underwear Run—a spinoff of the Underpants Run that takes place each year at Kona.

They gather outside the Lake Placid Pub on Mirror Lake Drive (get the Reuben if you go) at 10 a.m., strip down, put on funny hats, do their light run, and return to Lake Placid Pub to drink beer. They convey the opposite aura of the super serious athletes running the Ironman: a demeanor more *Bachelor in Paradise*, less *Ozark*.

I asked myself in that moment, "Why don't you do that one instead? They're all smiling. They're drinking beer. They're probably all going to have sex with each other after lunch. People all around you are vomiting, and you're clinging for dear life to the toilet roll dispenser of a porta potty so you can prop yourself up for your 449th dump of the race." Sometimes life just doesn't make sense.

By that point, I had seen eight people throw up during the run. It reminded me of a 3 a.m. Saturday morning walk at Providence College after a night of keg stands and shots. It wasn't a stretch to think I might be joining them sometime in the next eight miles.

Vomiting in the Marathon du Medoc makes sense to me. In fact, I'd say that if you don't vomit, you didn't do it right. Throwing up there would mean you got your money's worth. But watching runners pull off the Lake Placid course and lean over with their hands on their knees while they hurled a gallon of chunky Gatorade didn't have the same je ne sais quoi.

In addition to witnessing vomiting, it is not uncommon to see runners with bloody shirts. This happens when they forget to lubricate or put a preemptive Band-Aid on their nipples, and the friction from the jostling shirt over the course of twenty-six miles shreds those sensitive little appendages.

Researchers at the University of Durham conducted a study that concluded that runners who wear red clothing are more likely to win during competitions. The study determined that the color red signals dominance and higher testosterone levels.[2] I wondered if the large red circular blood stains that I now had on my shirt from my bleeding nipples

---

2   "Wearing red can make you appear angry and dominant," Durham University, May 13, 2015, https://www.dur.ac.uk/news/newsitem/?itemno=24710.

because I forgot to slather them in Vaseline at T2 were signaling dominance.

TIP: Put lubricant and Band-Aids on your nipples before the run.

Mile 19 (133.4)

Where was the damn turnaround?

Miles 19–24 are the hardest miles of the run, where you'll start to fade, and you'll have to fight to keep pace. I was plodding along, looking for the turnaround on River Road. It seemed like it would never come. I was eager to begin the final push back into town and to the finish line. Out here in the hinterland of River Road, the generators were cranked up and the temporary lights were on, even though it was still light out. This section would be a dark, desolate place to be running after dusk, and I was glad I'd have no part of that. Good Lord!

Speaking of the Lord, I came upon Father Dan Callahan, the famous Iron Friar. He comes down from Toronto each year and does Lake Placid to raise money for local charities. This was his seventeenth Lake Placid Ironman. He also says the 5:30 p.m. Mass at St. Agnes Catholic Church the Saturday evening before the race, peppering his homily with race parables.

Uncle Bob and Aunt Connie always attend this mass, and I usually join them. This year, Father Dan told the parishioners about the cross he wears that depicts Jesus as the good shepherd and invoked Pope Francis's quote that shepherds should smell like their sheep. He was grateful to be able to suffer in the race with all of them, he said.

At the end of Mass, he called all the athletes to the altar to bless them. I shuffled up to the front of the church with about fifty other athletes and then stood while Father Dan and all the parishioners prayed that we would have a safe and success-ful day. Father Dan ended the prayer with a twist on the old familiar Irish blessing, something along the lines of this:

> *May the road be downhill and the wind be always at your back.*
> *May your swimming lanes be open and your gog-gles clear.*
> *May your knees hold up and your bike not get a flat*
> *May your nutrition be on point and your vomit-ing limited.*
> *May you finish the race safely with a smile on your face.*

"I loved your homily last night," I said as I pulled up alongside him. "Thank you for the blessing."

He thanked me, and we chatted about the race conditions and how our bodies were holding up. "Well, you got what you wanted," I said. "To smell like a sheep."

He did not find my humor as funny as I did. We ran together for about a mile, and while sheep would have smelled like Chanel next to us, for a moment, it felt like two guys just out for a leisurely three-mile jog.

It was nice to lose myself in conversation for a few minutes and forget about how bad I smelled and how much my legs hurt. As bad as I felt, though, Father Dan seemed to be struggling even more. "Well, at least we're almost done," I said.

"Thanks be to God," I added, because I'm an idiot.

"Oh no, not me," he said. "I'm still on my first loop." I immediately said a silent prayer: *Thank you God, that I'm not Father Dan right now.* I couldn't fathom being on my first loop and still having hours to go. I had planned to ask him to say a prayer for me to give me the strength to get through the last couple of miles, but I decided he needed the Lord more than me. I bid adieu and continued on, alone, godless.

TIP: Find a friend along the route to distract you or help motivate or pace you. A good conversation can make the time go by easier and help you forget temporarily about your aches.

Mile 20 (134.4)

My hamstrings started to feel like bacon left in the frying pan too long, and I feared they might crumble at any moment. To this point, my race had been long and full of errors, but somehow, I was still hobbling along.

Mile 21 (135.4)

In my research during training, I came upon a *New York Times* report that stated that Alzheimer's disease can be prevented through running. A study by Washington University scientists found that elderly mice put on a running program experienced less dementia than those that didn't run.[3]

My experience is that Ironman, in fact, induces dementia. At the moment, I was racking my brain, trying to remember why on earth I did these. And every time I finish a race, I forget the pain, the misery, the grind. Every time. During the race, whether I'm swimming, biking, or running, I say to myself, *I will never do this again. I've finally learned my lesson.* A day after the race, dementia has set in, and I've signed up for the next one.

Mile 22 (136.4)

The world record holder for the fastest mile run is Hicham El Guerrouj at 3:43. As I began the climb up the hill in front of the ski jumps, I was in danger of breaking the record for slowest mile. I'd also do it in 3:43, but it would be three hours, not minutes. the anti-Hicham. I walked up. Slowly. I could not run.

Jim had raved about the hill work his run coach made him do during training. He'd start with a one-mile warm-up run

---

3   Gretchen Reynolds, "How Exercise May Keep Alzheimer's at Bay," *The New York Times*, January 18, 2012, https://well.blogs.nytimes.com/2012/01/18/how-exercise-may-keep-alzheimers-at-bay/.

at a 9:30 pace. Then he'd run up a hill five times at marathon pace (the pace you plan to run on race day, which for Jim was 9:05). Run up the hill. Run down. Repeat. After the fifth climb, he'd do a two-and-a-half-mile loop thirty-five seconds slower than marathon pace. Then he'd run up and down the hill five more times at sub-marathon pace.

This reminded me of the stories I had heard for years about the infamous hills behind Gillette Stadium that Bill Belichick makes his New England Patriots run after grueling practices to build their stamina and give the players a competitive conditioning edge. As one former player said, "It definitely teaches you how to become comfortable with being uncomfortable. It's a beast."

That sums up the Ironman experience perfectly. It's a beast, and you have to manage being uncomfortable. You also have to build a strong foundation before the race, so that hills like the one by the ski jumps don't destroy you.

A typical marathon training period is twenty-two weeks. In that time, a recreational runner will have run a little over 600 miles before getting to the start line. My training period was about half that, and I think it would be stretching it to say I ran sixty miles during that time.

I didn't do any hill work, and my only interval training was playing soccer with the boys and basketball for an hour once a week. It wasn't enough. I hadn't built a strong enough foundation. Had I done so, I wouldn't be suffering as much as I was now.

TIP: Hire a run coach or find a good training program and follow it. I recommend QT2 Systems, which offers complete endurance event preparation from more than forty professional coaches. QT2 is one of the top training programs on the tri circuit today. There are also some good ones that are free. One popular program is from legendary coach and author Hal Higdon. Higdon offers free and paid interactive training programs for beginners and advanced and everything in between. Many of my running friends, including Jim, have used and benefited from Higdon's programs.

Mile 23 (137.4)

I made it up the ski jump hill and started my slow slog of a jog again. A woman standing on the side of the road held a sign that read, "Ironmen Are Sexy." I wondered if she'd still think Ironmen are sexy if she could smell me. Sex with me at that point would have been like having sex with a rancid trash bag. Women in general aren't looking for that.

In all honesty, sex and Ironman do not go well together. First, we're generally sweaty and smelly all the time. Second, we're always tired and sore.

When you have kids, the only chance for romantic time is after those little urchins go to sleep. The problem with this is when I'm training, I can't keep my eyes open beyond the kids' bedtime, and I often fall asleep during tuck-in. What's more, my quads and hamstrings are invariably shot, and there's the very real possibility that the act of sex might cause my whole body to begin convulsing in a giant muscle spasm. Frankly, Karoline would get more out of a Bloomingdale's mannequin with a banana tied to it.

I know all about the studies that show that running boosts sex drive—that two and a half hours of running per week increases testosterone levels by 15 percent in men, and that women experience greater arousal and orgasm due to increased blood flow. After all, this was part of my initial pitch to Karoline on the benefits of me doing an Ironman.

I hadn't seen any studies on what running for five hours in one shot after biking for 112 miles and swimming for 2.4 miles did for the sex drive, but I can say with certainty that it had the opposite effect. All my body wanted after a race was a soft, sexless bed. Maybe in a few weeks when I got the feeling back in my legs and didn't smell like left-out fish Karoline would benefit from my increased testosterone levels.

Mile 24 (138.4)

You take about 33,000 steps in a marathon. I had taken about 30,000 of them. And I was feeling every one of them. Common injuries experienced by runners are IT band syndrome, plantar fasciitis, runner's knee, shin splints, and Achilles tendinitis. As

I now faced the hardest part of the race—the uphill climb back into town—it felt like my lower body was afflicted with every single one of these. Unfortunately, the warranty on my legs expired at mile 14, so I was stuck with them.

I labored up the hills as the spectators called out my name and told me that I could do it. Little kids lined the route with their hands extended hoping to get a high five. I obliged, more excited than they were about it. What a trip to have kids lighting up because middle-aged, mediocre me extended my hand for a high five. Some adults too. I was a figure of great admiration! Was this what it felt like to be Tom Brady?

The crowds boosted me up the hills, and I made the right turn onto Mirror Lake Drive. Aunt Connie and my cousins shouted my name. I limped past the Lake Placid Pub, where drunk patrons hailed me as some conquering hero, like they were brothers greeting a wounded soldier arriving home from the war, like they loved me and that my success in this race had somehow made their dull cornhole existence brighter.

Less than two miles and a guy with a cup of beer in hand, running alongside me to give me a pep talk, was all that was standing between me and Ironman glory. Good thing, too, because my body had had enough. Thank God they had started serving chicken broth at the aid stations.

CHAPTER 21
IRONMAN—
IT DOES A BODY GOOD?

What's your prediction for the fight?
Prediction? Pain.
— Clubber Lang, *Rocky III*

If you want to understand the agony and suffering of an Ironman, watch the end. If you've never seen someone finishing an Ironman race, it sometimes looks like a ninety-five-year-old blind-drunk Irishman staggering out of a Boston pub at midnight on St. Patrick's Day.

He steps carefully and gingerly, making sure of his footing with each step. He staggers a little, sometimes needing to stop and hold on to something to steady himself before continuing. Body parts aren't working correctly, the signals from the brain short-circuiting before they get to the limbs.

Once the man crosses the threshold of his home, and makes it to his bed, he collapses, too drunk and unconcerned to undress or even take off his shoes. He wakes in the morning having pissed himself, smelling like swamp ass, and sore as hell from *something*—his multiple falls to the pavement the evening before unremembered.

He mutters profanities and curses his stupidity. He vows to never drink again. He has learned his lesson. The next night, he's back in the pub, doing it all over again.

Doing an Ironman gives you a similar experience.

At the end of 140.6 grueling miles, you lurch across the finish line, and someone props you up and they take your picture and hang a medal around your neck and then you can't climb stairs for the next three days or sleep because your legs are throbbing so much.

You say *never again*. But in short time, like a mother who has forgotten the pain of pushing out a ten-pound child after thirty hours of labor, you're signing up for next year's race. Ironman is a seductive siren.

If you want a good representation of the annihilation at the end of one of these, just hop on YouTube and watch Julie Moss's famous finish in 1982, or Sian Welch and Wendy Ingraham nearly kill themselves in the 1997 World Championship at Kona in a battle for…as the announcer intones with dramatic effect…*fourth place.*

Julie Moss was a physical education senior at Cal Poly San Luis Obispo when she decided to do Kona in 1982 as research for a thesis on exercise physiology.

The title of that thesis should have been: "How to Completely, Utterly, Irrevocably Destroy Your Body."

She was the women's leader when her body started shutting down in the last miles of the run—her arms and legs splaying awkwardly like a drunken duck, muscles failing and legs buckling as if she had advanced ALS. She struggles and staggers and falls down multiple times within one hundred yards of the finish line.

A few yards from the finish, the second-place woman passes her. It's hard to watch. But then, a different feeling. One of awe. Inspiration. Disbelief. Moss, having lost the chance to win, keeps going. At this point, in deep distress, she crawls toward the finish. It is one of the most famous race endings in history. Broadcast on ABC's *Wide World of Sports*, it put Ironman on the national map.

As for Welch and Ingraham, in the last one hundred feet of the race they were running like two injured pterodactyls, just feet from the finish, they crash into each other—now two bugs that have been zapped by Raid and are struggling in an almost epileptic seizure as the poison goes to work. They both crawl, delirious, to the finish line, where they are whisked away for medical attention. The incident is aptly named "The Crawl."

Then there's Ironman legend Paula Newby-Fraser hitting the wall near the finish at Kona in 1995. I'll let the announcers pick it up from here: "She's totally disoriented...this is the cruel reality of Ironman but she's going on...she's in desperate trouble...the seven-time champion in her final Ironman finds her body in turmoil...It is so uncomfortable seeing someone so dominant in the Ironman being totally dismantled by the same event."[1]

As Newby-Fraser staggers, legs wobbling, looking more like Marvis Frazier after Mike Tyson knocked him senseless, well-fed fans crowd around her and yell, "You can do it, Paula! You got it! Just put one foot in front of the other! Come on, Paula!" These same people look like they'd drive their Cadillac across the street to visit the neighbors rather than walk the fifty feet, and they're encouraging a woman who, at this point, doesn't know her name to just put one foot in front of the other.

"It's getting more frightening—Paula Newby-Fraser lying down in the middle of the road," the announcer says.

"She needs an ambulance," a spectator says.

Her fiancé rushes to the scene and yells frantically, "Get an ambulance right now! 911!"

"I think I'm going to die," the thirty-three-year old mumbles as she proceeds to lie down on her back on the ground for twenty minutes. It's a scary scene. Then, somehow, miraculously, she convinces everyone that she's okay and gets up and walks barefoot the final 400 yards to the finish.

Paula was not just some Ironman novice who didn't know what she was doing. She had won Kona an unprecedented seven times! She had won an obscene *twenty-four* Ironman

---

1   DayofSuffering, "Paula Newby Frazier is 'Hitting The Wall' 1995 Ironman Hawaii," YouTube, September 22, 2009, https://www.youtube.com/watch?v=g_utqeQALVE.

races overall. She was a legend, an athletic machine. If someone so dialed-in and experienced like Newby-Fraser could end up looking like a punch-drunk boxer, then God help the rest of us attempting this physiological torture chamber.

You'd think watching these moments in Ironman history would prompt people like me to wise up. Somehow, they seem to have the opposite effect. I can still hear my wife's words after I showed her the videos on YouTube. "That looks fun to you? You're stupider than I thought."

There are medical tents at the finish of every Ironman, and they look like refugee camps for spandex-clad soldiers who just trudged thousands of miles across the desert. You could walk into any one of these makeshift medical facilities after a race and find every one of the 200 beds full of delirious, dehydrated athletes all hooked up to IVs.

Did Karoline have an argument, like wives of wealthy weekend climbers who decide to tackle Everest, did?

> *"Don, for god's sake please don't do this. The highest peak you've climbed is Mount Katahdin on our family vacation last summer. You're going to be climbing 23,000 feet higher! You're not ready!"*

> *"Poppycock, Dear. I'll hire a Sherpa to carry my stuff. I'll be fine."*

*"Don, people die every year climbing Everest! I'm
begging you!"*

*"If that is my fate, I gladly accept it to be able to
join those proud few who have summited Everest.
But don't worry, Poopsie, I promise I'll be fine.
Hey where are you going?"*

"I'm leaving you. I'm driving to my mother's."

*"Honey, you can't go right now. It's dark and it's
raining out. The roads are much too dangerous."*

"Fuck you."

What happens to the body during an Ironman to cause such
carnage? What makes my wife's send-off words "do not die" a
legitimate request?

Here's one fun fact: if you're contemplating doing an
Ironman, you should know that you will age twenty years.
You heard that right. All of you who have been searching for
the fountain of age, look no further—you've found it.

In the up to seventeen hours it takes to complete an
Ironman, an athlete's body decays two decades, going through
a physiological deterioration not unlike when the bad guy in

Indiana Jones and the Last Crusade drinks from the wrong chalice and goes through one heck of a backslide, winding up a pile of dust and bones in a matter of seconds.

Or for those parents with kids who have seen *Tangled* a hundred times, picture Rapunzel's mother, who experiences a similar time-lapse journey to infirmity and ashes as soon as Flynn Rider cuts the magic hair that had given her eternal youth.

This is essentially what happens to your body when you do an Ironman, where a forty-something-year-old at the beginning of the race ends it with the body of a sixty-something-year-old. The only thing missing is a Grail knight at the finish line intoning ominously, "You chose poorly."

How does this happen? A potpourri of exciting physiological wonders—dehydration, fuel supply shortages, muscle damage, brain fatigue, and overheating among them.

If you saw the HBO series *Chernobyl*, you'll recall the Soviets working feverishly to keep Reactor Core 3 from overheating and causing a horrific nuclear reaction. This precarious situation was caused by poor training, inherent reactor design flaws, and the disabling of safety systems. An ill-prepared Ironman's body is Reactor Core 3 in this scenario—one bad decision away from a complete meltdown.

Inside Triathlon magazine detailed some of what happens to the body during an Ironman in an exhaustive 2009 study. At the molecular level, oxygen radicals rip unapologetically through muscle cell membranes, mitochondria burn up glucose and triglyceride molecules, and blood rushes through veins and arteries like the Millennium Falcon going into hyperdrive.

During a race, your muscles expend more energy than Florida air conditioning units in August, constantly pushing heat out of the body. The most visible aspect of this is sweat, a vital cooling mechanism for the body.

TIP: On a warm day, an athlete will lose more than twenty pounds of fluid through sweat during the bike and run alone. Make sure you're replacing that fluid by drinking enough water and sports drink or you'll become dehydrated and end up like Newby-Fraser. I recommend Gatorade Endurance Formula. I also recommend you use it during training to get your stomach acclimated to it.

No matter how much you drink or eat during an Ironman, however, you can expect to lose about 5 percent of your body weight by the end of the race. The average Ironman competitor burns around 8,000 calories over the 140 miles. I generally lose about seven pounds.

In addition to sweating to keep the body cool, the brain also acts as a regulator and sends signals of fatigue and discomfort to force you to slow down if your body is drifting past the maximum safe core body temperature of 104 degrees.

But, according to *Inside Triathlon*, sometimes the brain itself overheats and doesn't function properly. This causes the central nervous system to break down and the athlete to become dizzy, disoriented, and uncoordinated to the point of collapse. Or Ozzy Osbourne in the twenty-first century.

Aside from your standard overheating and dehydration issues, your muscle tissues will go through a day-long MMA cage match, muscle cells being pulled, torn, and broken in a constant tug of war. This damage is from the mechanical stress of your muscles taking a brutal pounding, especially during the run.

Then there is oxidative stress, which happens when mitochondria release energy and oxygen molecules lose an electron, becoming oxygen radicals that then steal an electron from a healthy cell. The resulting free radicals wreak havoc on cells, DNA, and other proteins. In an endurance event the length of an Ironman, the production of oxygen radicals increases dramatically, resulting in ruptured muscle cells and serious muscle damage.

Then there is something called catabolism, which sounds a lot like cannibalism. Fitting, since this is the process where the body essentially eats itself to produce energy because there are no carbohydrates left to break down into glucose. This typically happens, as one online biochemistry dictionary points out, "when a person has not eaten in a while, such as during a period of famine or starvation." So if you want to know how your body would respond to a famine, just sign up for an Ironman. What a wonderful education you can get!

Here's the process, in a nutshell:

During an Ironman, the glycogen stored in the muscles and liver depletes as the day goes on. Glycogen, made from glucose molecules from the food you eat, is mainly stored in your liver and muscles. Your body mobilizes glycogen when it needs fuel. You cannot finish an Ironman without reserves of glycogen in the liver and muscles—when glycogen runs out, you're done. It's known affectionately as bonking.

When that happens, your adrenal glands will kick in and secrete the stress hormone cortisol, which will help break down carbohydrates and proteins to release energy. If there are no carbohydrates, i.e., no source of glucose, the amino acid molecules of the muscles will be broken down into carbon skeletons. Catabolism.

Then these molecules can be reconfigured and combined in a process called gluconeogenesis to create new glucose, as opposed to glucose that is broken down from glycogen stores from food sources. The cells can then use the new glucose as energy.

When your body starts to smell like ammonia, then you know it's in a cannibalistic...sorry, catabolic state, burning muscle protein to help you finish the race. This takes quite a toll on your muscles and contributes to the muscle damage that occurs.

TIP: If you feel you are hitting the proverbial wall and about to bonk, stop and eat some simple carbohydrates that can be rapidly absorbed. The best sources are sugary drinks such as sports drinks like Gatorade or Powerade, fruit juice, or an energy gel washed down with lots of water to get it into your bloodstream quickly. Energy bars and solid foods are full of complex carbohydrates and take longer to process, so they are less helpful during a bonk.

Finally, as I was experiencing firsthand, completing an Ironman is torture on your gastrointestinal system, and a full range of GI distress—everything from minor stomach discomfort and bloating to full-on diarrhea and/or vomiting—is available to you.

This is an especially likely outcome if, like me, you eat and drink too much before and during the race, or if you eat foods that are too difficult to digest. The body cannot tolerate what it usually can in your normal eating activities, and the rule of thumb is the more you take in, the more likely it will come out in ways you don't want.

If a person described all of these physiological and bio-chemical reactions and the body's severe impairment at the end of an Ironman and said they were the result of a bite from a black mamba or swallowing rat poison or getting struck by lightning or working at Chernobyl in May of 1986—it would be totally believable.

Yet you don't see thousands of people signing up year after year to participate in nuclear radiation tests. There is only one conclusion: people who keep doing Ironmans are lunatics.

By the way, don't worry about aging during the Ironman—the years are returned to you after a few weeks as your body heals. That is, unless you get sick like Jim did after Ironman Boulder. His body was so run down and his immune system so weakened after nine months of intense training topped off by the actual race in Boulder that he got shingles and meningitis right after the race.

It took four months for his body to return to normal. Jim's experience is common, and not surprising considering the outrageous stress you just put on your immune system—which is now being asked to fight off multiple foreign invaders and viral and bacterial infections after it just got the shit kicked out of it for seventeen hours following nine months of overexertion, lack of sleep, and abuse.

All things considered, it's a miracle every Ironman finisher doesn't come down with some debilitating sickness or crippling injury. Lunatics.

CHAPTER 22
THE (NOT SO) LONG-SUFFERING WIFE

When a girl marries, she exchanges the atten-
tions of many men for the inattention of one.

— Helen Rowland

Hi. This is Karoline. I thought I should have some say about all this, so here is my contribution to Russell's examination of the world of Ironman.

I try not to take it personally that Russell waited until we got married before he decided to tackle the illusive (and insane and brutal and life-sucking and bank account-draining) Ironman.

On July 2, 2011, Russell and I got married. We had a gorgeous reception in my parents' backyard on the Potomac River. We were surrounded by our closest friends, and our two huge families merged. Dinner was incredible. The band was even better. Our evening was even capped off with the most spectacular fireworks display I've ever seen. We were so in love. And happy. And ready to start our lives together. Birds were singing. Stars were aligning—all that lovey-dovey storybook crap. Life was perfect.

On July 24, 2011, Russell heard the call of a new siren by way of the Lake Placid Ironman. We hadn't even been on our honeymoon yet when he and his buddy, Jim, decided to camp outside in tents in the pouring rain so that, the next day, they could voluntarily stand in the summer heat for hours, passing out water and giving shoulder rubs to sweaty, exhausted Ironman racers in hopes that they, too, would have a chance to squeeze into spandex singlets and destroy their bodies through grueling exercise for thirteen hours straight the next year. Fun plan.

From the minute Russell told me they'd successfully signed up for Lake Placid 2012, I knew he was hooked. From that point forward, Russell's affections would be split between me and his pursuit of Ironman glory. And also with Jim, on whom he became increasingly dependent. Jim was equally hell-bent and crazy, yet much more organized and disciplined. Without Jim, I know Russell never would have embarked on this bizarre journey. It's also been Jim, however, who's helped tame Russell's natural recklessness and kept him safe and alive through the races over all these years.

Of course, it shouldn't have surprised me that Russell latched onto this Ironman idea and dove in head-first. He's a passionate guy—it's part of what I love about him. He finds something he likes, fully immerses himself in it, and does not let go. Period. And the more he learns about something, the more desperately he wants to be a part of it. The more people doubt him or dissuade him from his goal, the more aggressively he goes after it.

There was a time, after all, when I was his Ironman race. I know how cheesy that sounds, so please bear with me while I go down this sappy road....

Russell and I met in Baghdad when I was a public affairs officer and captain in the U.S. Air Force. I was deployed supporting Operation Iraqi Freedom, and Russell was there as a civilian contractor supporting the U.S. Army. We worked in the same office but not on the same team.

At the time, I had a boyfriend. We'd been on-again, off-again for a few years. Things were far from perfect, but we had decided to give long-distance a try.

Russell and I became friends quickly. For me, it was nothing more than that. Sure, we had a lot in common and had fun together, but I was trying to make it work with someone else.

Little did I know that Russell was developing feelings and seeking advice from family and friends. Most told him to back down. "She's got a boyfriend. She'll only break your heart," and, "You're barking up the wrong tree. Find someone else," or (my personal favorite), "OK, so she's a Baghdad 10, but more like a 6 when you get back to DC." (Yes, someone actually told him that.) I, too, did my best to make my intentions clear, keep it platonic, and put him firmly in "the friend zone."

And yet, Russell persevered. Our friendship became closer. We started going for runs together every day. We'd enjoy a cup of decaf and a chat after dinner every night. He went to "combat Catholic Mass" with me every Sunday. He listened attentively as I talked about my five brothers and sisters, friends, and hopes for the future. He comforted me when I was scared and encouraged me when I was doubting myself.

Every morning, he would pick up a pack of my favorite gum and leave it waiting for me on my computer keyboard. He even found a way to have a gorgeous bouquet of flowers delivered to me in the middle of Iraq on my birthday. It became impossible not to fall in love with him. (I told you this was sappy.)

Long story short(ish), as soon as I left Iraq, I broke up with the other guy (it was never going to work), and Russell and I officially started dating. Six months later, we were engaged, and ten months after that, we were married. His perseverance certainly paid off.

Knowing his personality and inability to back down, I was certain Russ was going to make this Ironman thing happen, come hell or high water. It didn't matter how often his Uncle Bob told him he lacked the discipline and proper training to safely compete or that Jim constantly teased him for having the wrong equipment. (He thought it unwise that Russell's plan for the bike-portion of his first Ironman to be a woman's loner bike that he'd never ridden before.)

It didn't matter that Russell's mom experienced massive anxiety at the thought of him drowning in the swim portion of the race. It didn't even matter that I kept reminding him that we were newlyweds, and he was wasting his energy during our honeymoon phase on training instead of quality time *(wink wink)* with his wife. He was laser-focused on making it happen.

I knew prepping for this race was going to be a big-time commitment and potentially dangerous, but I went along with it anyway. What choice did I have? I love my husband and don't want to hold him back. Plus, he told me he just wanted to do one to check it off his bucket list and to get it out of his system. Naively, I believed him.

Spouse-Tip: If your significant other says they want to participate in "just one" Ironman race, they're lying. Despite the time, pain, and cost, completing an Ironman is a high that can't be replicated. As soon as they're finished and no longer feel shooting pain in their legs, feet, and spine, they will want to go back for more. Congrats—Ironman is now a part of your relationship. Buy yourself an "Ironman Support Crew" fanny pack.

I feel this is an appropriate place to insert a disclaimer: Russell is a great guy. He's a good son and brother, caring husband, amazing father, and has more friends than anyone I've ever known. And I love him a lot. That said, the "Ironman crap," as I so lovingly call it, grew and grew through the years and at points became all-consuming.

Mind you, it's not as if Russell is a retiree in the post-work, post-young children chapter of his life who has nothing to do but train, race, and repeat. Instead, Russell's "Ironman phase" came during an otherwise extremely busy time in our lives. In the same seven years that Russell trained for and completed five Ironman races, we moved coast to coast twice, bought two houses and sold two houses, started six new jobs between the two of us and—most significantly—had three children. Oh, and I did manage to run one 5K. Go me!

Needless to say, it has caused a bit of unpleasant strain on our relationship. On more than one occasion, it's been disruptive to our lives and has been the spark that ignited a few arguments.

Here are some of my (least) favorite examples of how the Ironman has been a little bit life-ruiny:

- For our one-year anniversary, Russell booked us a one-night stay at an inn on Catalina Island. When we arrived, we were supposed to go out for a fancy celebratory dinner. Russ nonchalantly announced that he had to jump in his wetsuit for a "real quick" training swim first. After an hour getting ready and then an hour and a half swimming in Avalon Bay (which we later learned is literally some of the most polluted water in North America), he was too tired and it was too late for a nice dinner, so we grabbed snacks at the town grocery store, ate in our room and called it a night.

- After spending three hours one Sunday in ninety-degree heat while seven months pregnant trimming rose bushes at our house in Santa Clarita, California, I suggested we bite the bullet and spend $72 a month to hire someone to help maintain our small yard. Russell protested hard, insisting it was too much money and that he could do it himself. (He never did.) The next weekend, he proudly declared that he'd saved $3,000 by buying a $5,000 top-of-the-line road bike for only $2,000. That's right, only $2,000. Only $1,136 more than an entire year's worth of professional yard work....

- He stood next to me looking in the mirror in our bedroom while I was nine-months pregnant with our third child. I looked like a blotchy, bloated puffer fish and felt like the least attractive human on earth. Russell—now in training mode—rubbed his tiny, toned belly and said, "God, I'm getting really fat. I need to lay off the sugar and increase the intensity of my workouts." If death stares were daggers....

- The two of us were out on a very rare date night to celebrate my birthday after we'd just moved cross-country. At the time, we were living in a hotel with two kids under three, both starting new jobs, trying for a third baby, and attempting to buy a house when—after swearing up and down that he was done with Ironman—Russell declared he wanted to start training for yet another Ironman. Tears were shed. Eyes were rolled.

▪ And—the lowest point on this whole Ironman adventure—when he signed up and trained for the Chattanooga Ironman all the while intentionally keeping it a secret from me.

Right about now, I imagine you're thinking something like this, *"Surely, you're joking, Karoline. No husband in his right mind would spend thousands of dollars on registrations and equipment and plan a five-day weekend away from his family to run a race where 1) you could legitimately be seriously injured and 2) just two months prior had promised your wife you wouldn't run again all while keeping said wife in the dark."*

Well, that's exactly what happened.

Let me take you back to Lake Placid in July 2018 when Russell completed his fourth full Ironman. Due to unforeseen circumstances (almost crapping himself to death in the water after an ill-advised cayenne pepper shot before the swim, as you no doubt recall), his overall race time was not as good as it could have been. Still, he finished and made it back alive, so I was thrilled.

We normally spend a week with his family on Cape Cod every summer. That year, I did it by myself with all three kids so he could run the Ironman interruption-free. He promised time and again, before and after the race, that it was his last. It was too much money. He wanted to be present for vacations. He wanted to spend more time with the kids. He didn't want us to plan our lives around his races. The Ironman chapter was closed. I could breathe a sigh of relief.

I should have known better. Russell is uber competitive (mostly with himself) and once he gets an idea in his head he can't back down. He was already in great shape, and he knew he could have a stronger race. Jim and his other buddies were already signed up for Chattanooga at the end of September, and the race wasn't full yet. It was his chance to redeem himself after the Lake Placid blunder.

Rather than face my disappointed frown, an argument or—God forbid—tears, he decided to sign up in secret. He'd asked if he could go down to watch the race and support Jim, which I readily agreed to (naive young fool!). When he continued biking to work (something I knew he hated) and got super annoyed when I suggested he drive down for only two days to watch the race instead of five, I grew suspicious.

The night before he was supposed to go to Tennessee, I followed my hunch and pulled up the Ironman tracker app on my phone. I typed in his name and—sure enough—his bib number for the Chattanooga Ironman popped up. I was livid.

In that moment, I had to decide whether I should just kill him or confront him and work through it as a couple. While I'm sure a jury would have sympathized with me, I decided that on the off chance I was convicted and sent to prison, it would be unfair to my children to leave them parentless.

And, so, I confronted him. I've never seen such a guilty face or heard a man (especially *this* man) admit his mistake and apologize so quickly. Lots of tears. Lots of questions about our relationship. Lots of repeating of the phrase, "It's not about the race. It's about trust and respect." It brought up issues I never thought we'd face as a couple. It made me question myself. Was I really such a difficult wife that he'd rather lie to me than face a tricky conversation?

Copy and repeat a version of that same conversation for several nights—and weeks—to follow. Some nights, I think Russell would have preferred I follow through with my original plan and just put him out of his misery.

Fast forward to a year later, and I'm happy to say we made it past that hurdle and we're stronger for it. Even after the crap he pulled with Chattanooga, I gave my blessing for him to run another Ironman (am I generous or what?!). I also have full confidence that Russell will never sign up for a secret Ironman again (at least not if he plans to stay a married man).

Spouse-Tip: Don't lie to your wife and tell her that you're going to watch a buddy run an Ironman when you're actually planning to run an Ironman yourself. She's not dumb. She'll figure it out. And it will blow up in your face.

At this point, you might think I'm a bitter, jaded wife who's constantly angry at her husband for pursuing his dreams. Or, worse yet, a pushover who lets her husband walk all over her, dodge his responsibilities, and waste money while she sits at home all alone, sobbing while watching as the children destroy the house and call the pizza delivery guy "Dada" because Russell is always off training.

Fortunately for both of us, neither of those scenarios is true. In fact, there are a number of truly great things that have come from the Ironman chaos—despite the pitfalls—that have made it an overall positive experience for our family:

- Russell is setting an amazing example for his kids. He's an older dad (he was forty-two when the first of our three kids was born) and wants to stay fit, young, and healthy so he can keep up with them. I know that's a driving force behind these races. And, the kids see that his hard work pays off. Our oldest son proudly announces to anyone who will listen that his daddy is like a superhero because he's an Ironman and can do anything. Russell also involves the kids in training whenever possible. He puts them in the bike trailer for training rides. He often pushes our baby in the jogging stroller when out for runs. He shows the kids how to stretch and do pushups and make protein smoothies. They mimic him and understand what it means to be healthy. Our three-year-old middle son is already plotting his first Ironman race when he's eighteen. (Lord, help me!)

- Because of the Ironman competitions, I've seen some amazing places and met some amazing people. Lake Placid is gorgeous and a damn-near magical little town, and I never would have had a reason to visit if not for Russell's Ironman. The Ironman community is also very tight-knit and supportive. Other racers and their family members and friends are so encouraging and enthusiastic. It sucks you in and inspires you. The energy on race day is unmatched. Watching racers triumphantly cross the finish line at midnight after a seventeen-hour battle (plus months or years of training beforehand) in the water, on their bikes, and on the ground is one of the most beautiful and emotional experiences I've ever had in my life.

- Through it all, Russell shows me time and again that family is his priority. Even when a race is two weeks out, and he should be putting everything into training, if one of our kids is sick or has a bad dream, he will stay up all night with them. He's put off training runs to attend school shows. He's broken his race diet to take me out for nice dinners. He'll skip a training day all together if one of my cousins or college friends comes into town for a visit. Ironman may be an obsession, but I know family will always come first.

- My pride in Russell has grown by leaps and bounds. Every time he runs a race, I see the passionate guy I fell in love with. I'm in awe that he keeps a smile on his face throughout each grueling mile and makes almost freakishly quick recoveries. I see that he is strong and confident and can literally do anything. He inspires me to aim higher and work harder.

Yes, the Ironman and I have a love-hate relationship. It's been a big and sometimes wonderful part of our marriage and family life. That said, if Russell decides soon to move on from the Ironman competitions, I won't be at all disappointed. I keep encouraging him to take up something a little less intense like golf or tennis or Netflix bingeing. With my luck, as soon as he closes the Ironman chapter for good, he'll decide to pursue something bigger and crazier. Like Everest. Or free solo rock climbing.

Sweet Jesus, I hope I haven't just given him any ideas....

CHAPTER 23

FINISH LINE

*My goal was always to cross the finish line with nothing
left, and if I did that, I really didn't care what anybody
else had done. I had been successful, I had satisfied
my desire to do well at this race, and if it was a gold
medal, it was great; if it was tenth place, it was just as
good because I'd learn something about my ability.*
— Eric Heiden, Olympic Gold Medalist,
1980 Winter Olympics, Lake Placid

Miles 25–26.2 (139.4–140.6)

I bounded down Mirror Lake Drive. Less than a mile to go.
Somehow, someway, this was not going to be a Julie Moss
finish. I've always been able to sprint the last hundred yards.
Clearly, I should be pushing myself harder. Clearly, I ignored
Eric Heiden's words to finish with nothing left. There would
not be a gold medal for me.

But if I came down the track staggering and slobbering
like Moss, Welch, or Ingraham, Karoline would NEVER let
me do another one.

If I finished like Paula Newby-Fraser in 1995, looking like
a punch-drunk boxer, it would scare my mother to death, and

she'd find a way to file a restraining order to keep me from setting foot anywhere near an Ironman race ever again.

If I ended up like Uncle Bob's friend Karen, delirious, dehydrated, and drooling on herself, sitting shell-shocked in a lawn chair for forty minutes like she just came from the war, my Ironman days would be over.

Someday maybe I'd go there and push it. But not today. Bob's number one goal and his constant advice to me is to finish happy and healthy. Unlike the pepper shot, it's perfect advice.

I had witnessed the triage that happens in the medical tent. I had watched the carnage. I had seen a woman desperately trying to find a porta potty, nasty brown fluids pouring down her legs. I didn't want to spend my finish lying on a bed hooked up to an IV of saline and sugar water. I wanted to spend it at Chimex hooked up to an IV of Dos Equis.

The cowbell-clanking crowds whooped and cheered me on. "You've got this, Russell! You're going to be an Ironman!" Jim, Mark, and Jeff had abandoned their post. They'd be at the finish line. I entered the Oval, site and symbol of so much Olympic glory. By now, I was sprinting. Where was this energy earlier? Nothing was sore at that moment. This was not a Julie Moss finish. I was strong.

The crowd screamed. I felt like an Olympian. Overcome, tears began to roll down my cheeks. It all came out. I was going to do it. During the swim, I didn't think I would. Impossible.

What a feeling! Maybe it's the same feeling a parent has at a child's college graduation or wedding. When you've sacrificed so much and worked so hard to come to a moment—a wedding, a graduation, a first birth. It's hard to describe, but I can't help crying. Every time.

I was going to finish. All my inadequacies, all my failures, they didn't matter. All the things about myself that I wasn't proud of, so many shortcomings and flaws, receded. I was blessed with health and a body that allowed me to do something so utterly grueling, so mentally and physically taxing that it was incomprehensible to most humans. It was enough.

Jim, Mark, and Jeff were stationed along the barrier right before the finish. They were beaming and hooting and yelling. I was blessed with friends who loved me and cared about me—who would celebrate my success as if it were their own. It was more than enough.

I crossed the finish line, arms extended to the sky, exalted, and let out a warrior scream. *"Russell Newell, you are an Ironman!"* Mike Reilly announced. A volunteer wrapped a foil blanket over me.

I had been in the arena, face marred by dust and dirt and sweat. The past six months, nine months really, had been worth it for this moment. The great exhale. The deluge down my cheeks. I had dared greatly and strived valiantly and knew the triumph of high achievement, one that most would never know. I belonged to a special club, an admired tribe of crazy warriors.

"Congratulations! Do you need medical attention?" the volunteer asked.

"No, I'm good." Another volunteer hung a medal around my neck and whisked me toward a backdrop with the Ironman logo to take a photo of me with my medal—a medal that my three kids would look upon with awe and wonder, as if it accorded me superhero status, equal in their eyes to their respective favorites, Spiderman and Batman. How could I ask for anything more?

The volunteer walked me down the chute to the boxes of pizza set up on tables. I had not been hungry and didn't eat much during the last half of the run, but I was ravenous now.

I was already thinking about Chattanooga. So many things to improve. Would I come back to Lake Placid to do another one? Yes. Absolutely, yes. Positively. I would. The lure of… everything…was too great.

"All right," she said. "I'm going to leave you now. Are you okay?"

"Yeah, I'm great…I'm an Ironman," I said. Unbowed and unbroken. Triumphant and exuberant. "I'm a god-damn Ironman."

Finis

ACKNOWLEDGMENTS

Linda Marrow—for your guidance, coaching, cheerleading, editing, wisdom, and belief in me. Bob Falconi—for introducing me to Ironman and for your generosity with advice and so many other things. Connie Falconi and Lisa and David Perfield—for your kindness and for sharing the adventure for all these years. My Ironman crew: Jim Kane, Mark Bergeron, Kara Bergeron, Diane Stokes, Jeff Hojlo, Stephen Desio, Mary Sullivan—thank you for your friendship, advice, ideas, equipment, jokes, meals, and for sharing the grind and elation of Ironman. Tim Snow and Beth Shutt with QT2 Systems—for allowing me to join your 2018 Ironman Lake Placid breakfast and for sharing advice and wisdom on nutrition and training. Sarah Mills of SoMoved Nutrition—for teaching me so much about nutrition and diet and helping me get my body ready for Ironman Lake Placid and Ironman Maryland in 2018. Mom and Dad—for everything, including good genes. Peter, Fintan, Nora, and Fiona—for the pure joy you bring me as your dad.

ABOUT THE AUTHOR

Author photo by Paco Hamm

A critically acclaimed author, former writer for Disney-ABC Television, and six-time Ironman, Russell Newell plunged into the world of Ironman triathlon in 2012 at Lake Placid and has explored every cutting-edge nutritional supplement and muscle recovery tool to coax his creaking body to get out of bed each morning to swim, bike, and run. He has sought every aerodynamic adjustment and equipment edge to beat his archrival, Jim Kane, in a series of races more fraught than the last ones. With a very accommodating wife, three young kids, and a baby on the way, he's continued to race these torturous, bank account-sucking, narcotic-level addicting affairs, while poorly trying to balance his family life. His book, *Irondad Life*, explores *just* how poorly.